Stupid Moments

Stupid Moments

*62 Revealing Stories
About Those Sensitive Times
and What We Learn from Them*

COMPILED AND EDITED BY YVONNE LEHMAN

BROKEN ARROW, OK

Scripture quotations marked NLT are taken from the *Holy Bible, New Living Translation*, copyright © 1996. Used by permission of Tyndale House Publishers, Inc., Wheaton, Illinois 60189. All rights reserved.

Scripture quotations marked NIV are taken from the *The Holy Bible, New International Version*. Copyright © 1973, 1978, 1984, International Bible Society. Used by permission of Zondervan. All rights reserved.

Scripture quotations marked NASB are taken from the New American Standard version of the Bible. Copyright © 1960, 1962, 1963, 1968, 1971, 1972, 1973, 1975, 1977, 1995 by The Lockman Foundation. Used by permission.

Scripture quotations marked NLT are taken from The Holy Bible. New Living Translation copyright© 1996, 2004, 2007, 2013 by Tyndale House Foundation. Used by permission of Tyndale House Publishers Inc., Carol Stream, Illinois 60188. All rights reserved.

STUPID MOMENTS

62 Revealing Stories About Those Sensitive Times and What We Learn from Them

ISBN-13: 978-1-60495-021-2

Copyright © 2016 by Yvonne Lehman. Published in the USA by Grace Publishing. All rights reserved. No part of this book may be reproduced in any form or by any electronic or mechanical means, including information storage and retrieval systems, without permission in writing, except as provided by USA Copyright law.

From Samaritan's Purse

We so appreciate your donating royalties from the sale of the books *Divine Moments, Christmas Moment, Spoken Moments, Precious Precocious Moments, More Christmas Moments* and *Stupid Moments* to Samaritan's Purse. What a blessing that you would think of us! Thank you for your willingness to bless others and bring glory to God through your literary talents. Grace and peace to you.

Their mission statement:
Samaritan's Purse is a nondenominational evangelical Christian organization providing spiritual and physical aid to hurting people around the world.

Since 1970, Samaritan's Purse has helped victims of war, poverty, natural disasters, disease, and famine with the purpose of sharing God' s love through his son, Jesus Christ.

Go and do likewise.

Luke 10:37

You can learn more by visiting their website at www.samaritanspurse.org

Dedication

Dedicated to
Terri Kalfas, who saw the beauty
and value of sharing praise in
Divine Moments
Christmas Moments
Spoken Moments
Precious, Precocious Moments
More Christmas Moments
and now makes it possible
for the sharing of
Stupid Moments

and

to all the brave souls who admitted
and shared their stories for this
compilation
regardless of personal embarrassment
and
without compensation
just for the thrill of being useful
and be part of the mission work of
Samaritan's Purse

Contents

Introduction 9
1. It Was You! *Sharon Blackstock Dobbs* 11
2. Napkins Don't Taste Good *Yvonne Lehman* 12
3. Order Clerk Blues *Alice Klies* 18
4. Green Goop Guilt *Gloria Spears* 20
5. But He's Just a Puppy, *Tommy Scott Gilmore, III* 23
6. Men or Women? *Elsie H. Brunk* 28
7. Sweet Memories *Debra DuPree Williams* 29
8. Raisin Br-ants *Susan Dollyhigh* 31
9. Swimming with the Fishes *Joann M. Claypoole* 32
10. Computers, Too? *Yvonne Lehman* 36
11. Give Me a Thrill *Karen Nolan Bell* 37
12. A Sordid Sunday Afternoon *Roger E. Bruner* 40
13. From 14-Karat Mind to the Mind of Christ *Vicki H. Moss* 43
14. Oops! *Jean Wilund* 48
15. Don't Ask! *Yvonne Lehman* 50
16. The Library Book *Dianna Beamis Good* 51
17. Toilet Tissue Tale *Audrey Tyler* 55
18. Leaders Gone Wild *Janet Bryant Campbell* 56
19. Does This Tube Make My Butt Look Big? *Lillian Humphries* 59
20. I'm Melting *Dr. Rhett H. Wilson, Sr.* 61
21. Prepared for Presentation *Dorothy Floyd* 64
22. I Got Confused *Diana Leagh Matthews* 65
23. The Internet Date and the 23rd Psalm *Jan Westmark* 67
24. Meow! *Yvonne Lehman* 70
25. The Prayer Stick *Gloria Anderson* 71
26. The Miracle Suit *Susan Dollyhigh* 73
27. Expensive Chocolate Milk *David A. Lehman* 76
28. My Momma Taught Me… *Cindy Sproles* 77
29. Not Exactly the Smartest Things *Tommy Scott Gilmore, III* 80
30. All Thumbs *Diana Flegal* 83
31. Front and Center *Maggie Micoff* 84

32. Surrender to Laughter *Debbie Presnell* 88
33. Let Them Eat Cake *Ann Tatlock* 90
34. Stupid or Pretty Smart? *Toni Armstrong Sample* 92
35. Do You Read and Write? *Yvonne Lehman* 95
36. I Could Have Been a Contender if I Hadn't Had a Jesus Crush
    Vicki H. Moss 97
37. Who Died? *Joye Atkinson* 102
38. iSwim at the Beach *Joann M. Claypoole* 103
39. Sir, Have You Been Drinking? *Nate Stevens* 107
40. A New Windshield *Barb Suiter* 110
41. All Shook Up *Yvonne Lehman* 112
42. How Stupid Can You Smile? *Donna Collins Tinsley* 114
43. Wonder Who's Calling? *Helen L. Hoover* 117
44. Look for the Signs *Andrea Merrell* 120
45. Riding Oatsie *Marybeth Mitcham* 122
46. Filled to the Measure *Susan Dollyhigh* 125
47. Bubba and the Bachelorette Party *Kathy Whirity* 127
48. Indecent Exposure *Mason K. Brown* 130
49. And You Teach What? *Theresa Jenner Garrido* 133
50. The Wrong Garden *Rebecca Carpenter* 135
51. Crash Landing *Colleen L. Reece* 137
52. Gee, I Wish I Could Get Tired *Tommy Scott Gilmore, III* 139
53. A Twisted Kiss *Terri Kelly* 142
54. Repeat After Me: I Am Not the Holy Spirit *Shelley Pierce* 145
55. Lawn 911 *Barbara Latta* 148
56. Maps Don't Trump a Sense of Direction *Sandra Merville Hart* 151
57. White House Calling *Alice Klies* 153
58. The Weight of Foolishness *Leigh Ann Thomas* 155
59. Focus Lost and Found *Lynn Lilja* 158
60. Me? Have A Stupid Moment? *Fran Lee Strickland* 160
61. The Closet Prayer *Yvonne Lehman* 162
62. A Place of Trust *Nick Harrison* 164
About the Authors 166

Introduction

When I was a little girl, my grandmother would plait my hair and send me off to school in pigtails. I didn't like that and would say, "I'm not pretty."

She would always say, "Pretty is as pretty does."

My thought was, *I don't "does" anything and that means I'm not pretty.*

Well, I decided to do something about that. When nobody would curl my fine, straight hair I learned to do it myself by rolling up wet strands of hair in brown paper sack strips, and sleeping in them. Never mind the head pain. I became one gorgeous kid who came out of her shell, shook her head to bounce her curls, and smiled. I was "does-ing" something pretty!

Another thing my grandmother said, after my older sister called me "stupid" and had to get a hickory switch for that, was, "Don't ever say that word." So I got the impression my sister had cussed me, and *stupid* was a cuss word.

Then, years later along came Forrest Gump, who said, "Stupid is as stupid does." His Momma told him that.

Uh oh!

He and his Momma used that cuss word, and frankly I'd thought it about myself a few…well, more than a few…times.

But if a little girl could do something about being pretty, maybe this mature woman could do something about being "that cuss word" since it had become a big part of my life.

Of course, the place to go is the Bible. And I found this verse in Proverbs 12:1 (NLT): To learn, you must love discipline; it is stupid to hate correction.

Therefore, if one behaves stupidly, it is stupid not to learn from it.

Although it's unacceptable to call others a word they find offensive, stupid is a valid word in the English language with definitions ranging from foolish, silly, laughable, to unwise or acting in a careless way.

I seemed to have permission from Momma, Forrest, the Bible, dictionary, and thesaurus to title a book *Stupid Moments*, but still…I could almost feel the sting of a hickory switch.

Until…one day while reading my morning devotion, I was absolutely shocked to read that Oswald Chambers — you hear that…Oswald Chambers — was disclosing a difficult time in his life and he wrote, "I seem stupid."

Oswald Chambers! A famous Christian, best known for his classic devotional *My Utmost for His Highest*. You can learn more about him in one of this book's articles.

Other stories in this book range from fun to faith, from the ridiculous to the sublime. Whether our actions are everyday foolish, silly, funny, embarrassing, or serious times that are faith based, and we feel…stupid…think of Oswald Chambers and know…we're in good company.

~ Yvonne Lehman

∼ 1 ∾

It Was You!

It was you;
You who didn't feed the cat,
Or lock up all the doors.
You who left the garbage the dog scattered on the floor.
You who left the milk to sour in the kitchen sink.
It was you.

You shrug your shoulders, raise your brows and say, "It wasn't me."
I know that look of innocence when you are in denial.
Finding all your hiding spots is a monumental trial.
Why can't you leave well enough alone and let it be?

Now, where have you put my glasses? My keys, where are they?
I search high and bending low I fall down on my knees,
My glasses slip onto my nose to the jingling of my keys.
Oh, well…
Maybe it was me.

∼ Sharon Blackstock Dobbs

❧ 2 ❧
Napkins Don't Taste Good

When my daughter was four years old she came into the house with her pretty little face screwed up as she said, "Worms don't taste good." The retelling of that incident has brought laughter to our family and friends for decades, even to the one who apparently tasted the worm. None of us were embarrassed about what she did; we found it entertaining.

I think of other incidents that generate laughter such as someone running into a door, missing a chair while attempting to sit, saying the wrong thing at the wrong time, twisting one's words, suddenly stumbling over nothing.

A friend and I had many hilarious times because of my being directionally impaired and even trying to get into the wrong car because types of cars don't register with me.

When we were traveling to a writer conference, she said, "Turn left at the next road." I turned…and stopped. Instead of turning onto the street she meant for me to drive down I had turned into a store's parking lot!

Entire movies and television shows make us laugh when people make blunders. Entertaining shows are filmed about blunders. The world's funniest videos are built around things going wrong. If the person survives, it's funny.

One story that stuck with me has brought surprise and laughter to many. In her newspaper column, Ann Landers wrote about a formal dinner she attended. She cut the item on her plate and began to eat it. Others stared and gasped until someone told her that was a napkin. She'd thought it was a cookie. She was never invited to another gathering by that hostess.

Obviously the mishaps, wrong words, slip-ups, mistakes, blunders, are humorous — until they happen to us. Yet even when we are humiliated and mortified, and the brunt of the so-called joke, after time passes we can often laugh about it.

After the blunder, we often receive good advice when we're expressing our humiliation or mortification over the blunder. We're told to think before we speak. Use common sense. Plan ahead. Be prepared. Be aware of danger. Do the simple, direct thing. Some may try and soothe us by saying, "They won't give you another thought."

That might be true if the joke is on us. But what can't be labeled funny or entertaining is when our blunder results in hurt feelings, awkwardness, or humiliation for another person.

That happened to me when my family had gathered at a restaurant to celebrate my granddaughter's having accomplished a swimming feat and upcoming departure for college. A couple who knew me came over to the table and the man said, "Is this your family?"

I introduced my granddaughter and began to tell of her recent accomplishment. My mind knew I shouldn't have raved on about her, so I then jumped to introducing the couple, which gave the impression the introductions were over. An awkward moment followed. I'd begun to cut my napkin and no one was laughing.

My senior moment, or inner censor, or something kept me from continuing to introduce my family. I'd mentally stuck a piece of napkin in my mouth.

The couple looked surprised and mumbled something about hoping we enjoyed the time together. They turned and walked away. My family sat silent.

I began chewing the napkin.

How I wish the couple had known me well enough to say something like, "Well, she can't even introduce her family," and laugh, then look at another family member and ask, "Who are you?" That could have been laughed about.

Or if a family member had the introduced her/himself. But that didn't happen. They each remained silent.

I swallowed but felt like I was choking on the napkin.

The couple could very well think I didn't want them to know my family. My family could think I didn't want to introduce them. I felt like I'd pulled into a parking lot and stopped instead of turning left and continuing down the road.

When I lamented to my family, the response was that they weren't offended and the couple would forget it.

One said, "Learn from it and don't do it again."

Don't do it again doesn't fit. I know how to introduce my family. I simply didn't do it. When something that should be simple becomes awkward, that's not funny.

I called the couple, got voice mail and left a message, apologized, explained I was caught up in my granddaughter's celebration, should have introduced my family, I was sorry, forgive me.

I know the couple will continue to be cordial and we might even try to laugh at the blunder. But I can never put the napkin back on the plate. The others cannot look at the napkin-eater without seeing the empty plate.

My blunder is minute compared with huge problems others are facing. But that doesn't mend what I did. Unintentional doesn't make it right. It's not funny when one eats her napkin.

There's a saying, "Eat your words." That means if you say something wrong, you have to admit you said something wrong. I have to admit I didn't say something right, which was to introduce my family.

I'm a professional writer and one might expect me to say the right things at the right time. However, writing is done on a computer screen. Words can be edited, changed, or deleted. When they come from the mouth, that's final. I can't edit myself, but at times wish I could punch the delete key.

Maybe somewhere along the line this may help someone, and me, to think…twice…three times…before speaking even when it seems to be a simple action of introductions when someone comes up and says, "Is this your family?"

There's nothing funny about eating one's napkin. It feels like worms crawling around in the stomach and they really don't taste good.

That could very well be the end of the story. The logical conclusion is that I would continue kicking myself mentally and emotionally, until time eased the humiliation.

But what happened on various days of the week taught me a lesson. Days of the week are important here. The humiliation with the couple happened on Wednesday. I called and left my apologetic message on Wednesday evening.

On Thursday, I wrote a letter to the couple, saying I didn't know why I didn't introduce my family and I included a paragraph of a brief introduction of them. Two family members said the couple would have dismissed it and I'd just stir it up again, so I didn't send the letter.

On Friday I wasn't feeling any better, so I edited the letter and explained about a writer's mind that sees a dozen possible answers when a question is raised and often chooses the wrong answer. I even mentioned my "faux pas" and my son said, 'Why are you speaking French? Just talk to them.'"

But then I felt crazier than ever and did not send the letter.

On Saturday, I decided to autograph one of my books to them and just say thank you for stopping by to meet my family and maybe I don't function well in the real world but at least I'm still into fiction.

That didn't help, so I didn't take the book to their home.

On Sunday, when I went to lunch after church with three friends I told them about the incident. They all said there was nothing I could do to make it better. Let it go! One said I had been caught up in wanting to make a good impression. I thought, yes that's true, but not any more than I'd want to make a good impression on anyone else. I introduce professional people at my writers conferences all the time.

Sunday afternoon I called a friend of the couple and related the experience and asked if there might be something to make the couple not feel offended. She said she wouldn't have given it another thought and the couple probably wouldn't, either.

Wednesday, Thursday, Friday, Saturday passed. I had prayed God would give me a way to make it right, even turn back the days so I could try again. After all, the Bible says he made the sun stand still one time! Well, of course he didn't turn back time for me.

On Sunday night, I changed the way I prayed about it. Everything I'd thought of doing might have helped me feel better. Any gesture I might make would likely end with the couple saying all was well. I knew they had a life beyond my not introducing my family.

So I prayed that God would forgive me for trying to do anything that would make Me feel better. I asked forgiveness for dwelling on it while people along the east coast were losing homes and lives due to Hurricane Irene. I asked God to help that couple know I didn't mean to slight them, didn't mean to be rude, didn't mean to cause a moment of discomfort. I asked God, tentatively, if he might do something to make this right, if he wasn't too busy with more important things. I really didn't expect anything. I was just trying to put an end to my misery.

On Monday, I went to lunch with a man and woman who were friends with me and my husband before he died. They had read in the newspaper about my granddaughter's recent accomplishment and wanted to take me out in honor of her. We had a wonderful time talking about places all three of us had visited such as Israel and Paris. We talked about family. I forgot my misery. Then when we were about to leave, in walked The Couple!!

My face must have shown what I felt, which was a lack of blood. The man said, "What's wrong?" I told them the story. All the while I was trembling, knowing God was giving me a face-to-face opportunity. And it shook me.

The man said, "Just go over and say 'It's good to see you. How are you?' That's all." So, with trepidation, I approached them. They were sitting with another couple. Before I could say anything, the man smiled and said, "You didn't need to make that phone call."

I said, "Oh, yes I did." I pointed to my head. "Had a brain lapse."

His words had eased the tension. He looked amused. I'd never seen him look amused. He said, "Don't worry about it."

They smiled.

I was glad The Couple didn't introduce the couple sitting with them. That was probably a deliberate omission or they figured I'd forget to say, "Nice to meet you."

I knew that face-to-face confrontation is what was needed. I'd never joked with that couple, but now whenever we see each other, we don't need to feel uncomfortable. I can now joke about myself, or just shake my head and they'll know what I mean.

But as my friends and I left the restaurant, I felt that overwhelming sense of God's presence. He orchestrated that, although it is minor if compared with the trials and devastation taking place in other lives.

When I returned home I consulted my calendar to see when certain events took place. On Wednesday, my granddaughter's picture and article about her swimming accomplishment were in the paper. On Thursday, my friends called to invite me to lunch.

God knew I was going to be anxious all week about my "faux pas." (God probably does speak French!) He was working out a way to ease any tension for me and the couple, even before I got around to praying about it the right way, before I knew I had to let go, give it up, and leave it to God if he wanted to do anything, because I was helpless.

I shouldn't be, but am amazed when I'm so aware God is present in the so-called small everyday things of life. His big miracles don't surprise me. Little things do.

I may eat a lot of napkins in this life, but the King has a way of reminding me he still has an open invitation for me to attend his banquet.

But you can bet, I'm not picking up a knife and fork until he gives the signal, and even then, I'm gonna look around…

~ Yvonne Lehman

❧ 3 ❧
Order Clerk Blues

"Hello, I'm here to apply for the order clerk position."

The man across from the rather ominous leather top desk, stood. "Welcome to Jobbers Warehouse. Tell me, do you know a lot about cars and engine parts?"

I actually didn't know if the motor was in the front or rear of a car. Didn't some of those cars that people called 'bugs' have an engine in the back?

"Yes, yes." I lied as I pulled on the hem of my skirt and fiddled with my purse. "My brother is four years older than me and he has been a great teacher." I glanced toward the ceiling. Maybe a bolt of lightening would strike me!

A week into the job, while I sat comfortably taking orders from auto parts stores, I received a call from one of our largest clients.

I answered the phone, "Jobbers Warehouse. This is Alice, may I help you?"

"I need some shoes." The voice on the other end was gruff and business like.

Without hesitation, I said. "I'm sorry sir, we don't carry shoes. You might try Sears." I placed the phone on its cradle and smiled. Silly man, didn't he know we sold auto parts.

A few minutes passed. My boss's private line rang into his office. A few seconds later, the buzzer beeped on my intercom. "Alice could you please come into my office?"

My boss motioned for me to sit in the chair in front of his desk. "Alice, did someone just call here asking for shoes?"

"Why yes," I felt my eyebrows lift to my hairline. I started to chuckle. "I referred him to Sears. I don't know who he thought we were."

My boss stood, pushed back his chair, and motioned for me to follow him. We walked toward a rear door to the warehouse. We meandered up and down several isles before he stopped. He pointed to a middle shelf. A large sign hung above a row of parts. It read, BRAKE SHOES.

My boss slapped his leg and howled with laughter. I threw my hands across my face. I didn't know whether I should laugh or cry. I sheepishly headed toward the office. By now the entire crew in the warehouse whistled and laughed out loud.

I made it my passion to learn every car part in the warehouse, but it didn't keep the crew from fondly calling me "Shoeless" for the next few years that I worked the job.

It also didn't help me erase the feeling that the word 'stupid' stood out on my forehead like a neon sign!

~ Alice Klies

☙❧

I said to my son, "Emily is having a genre party Saturday."
He said, "Why?"
I stated the obvious. "For the baby."
"I don't understand," he said.
"So we know if the baby is a girl or boy."
"Oh, you mean gender, not genre."
Yup! That's what I meant.
She's not having a novel, she's having a baby!

~ Yvonne

4
Green Goop Guilt

The sun shone through the clouds as I drove to my client's home. Thankful for my business that makes life easier for others in their everyday living, I smiled as I reflected on the beautiful spring day.

Shortly after being single again, I had discovered it was going to be hard financially. I needed to earn an income comparable to the lifestyle I was accustomed to when I was married. The job opportunities offered in our area's newspaper hadn't caught my interest, nor did the pay.

In my prayer time and journaling, the Lord impressed on my heart about starting an errands service in the tourist area where I live. I know the Lord is the creator of witty business ideas, and now I welcomed him as my witty business partner. Indeed, I needed his help and guidance daily and knew somehow he would provide.

My clients had recently returned from a beach trip and needed my services to get some shopping done. Grocery shopping, picking up their laundry and buying a few items at the drug store, were just a few things on a long list they had me. I was happy to be busy and knew they were satisfied with my services.

When I arrived at their home, my client, Chloe, met me at the door and asked if I would be interested in detailing her car, especially on the inside. The car mats were partly covered with loose grass and mud. The air vents were as dusty as mine were, which reminded me I needed to detail my own car. The interior, a rich beige leather, was nice, but had several stains. An unfamiliar odor permeated the car, but I couldn't decide what it was or where it was coming from.

Today it certainly didn't smell or look like a new car. Their trip had taken a toll on both the inside and outside. Their new car did need a good bath.

I told her I would be happy to give it a try. I didn't normally provide this service, but she had become a friend too, so I was confident and determined their car was going to be sparkling clean when I returned it.

I purchased the best package for washing the outside of the car. The friendly attendants were eager to assist and worked effectively as a team. They gave the car a good bath. One washed the rims and tires, one sprayed and cleaned each window, another washed the headlights with a long brush. The final run was through the automatic wash, which included the works.

The attendants followed me to the vacuum area. They came prepared with drying towels as they worked hard on finishing details. I was pleased when I walked around the car to inspect it. Good as new on the outside. Now my part to work on the inside. I was getting paid to detail Chloe's car and it was going to be good as new inside and out if it took me all day.

Several hours passed. Their car looked like a new car should look, inside and out. I sprayed the New Car Scent fragrance as the finishing touch. I was ready to return their shiny clean car.

But, I still noticed a slight odor. *What is that smell?* Maybe I sprayed too much fragrance? I rolled down the windows, turned the air conditioning fan on high, waited a few minutes, then rolled windows back up…but the smell still lingered. Looking down at the console, I realized it was the one place that I hadn't bothered to check. I quickly raised the lid. My eyes bulged as I took a closer look inside.

Yuk! What was that dried greenish gray stuff? Yes, my nose confirmed this was what I'd been smelling. But, no worries. Determined, I used some extra muscle power and a scrub brush, and the console was as good as new too!

Finally, this car was ready to go home. I glanced up in the rear-view mirror at myself. My face was flushed, my forehead sweaty, strands of hair stuck out from my ponytail. Now to finish the shopping and drive this clean car home.

When I pulled into the garage, Chloe heard me and came out to see the car. "Wow, it looks great!" she said.

I was pleased that she was happy with her clean car. I proudly opened the car door so she could see the inside too. She was amazed at the difference.

I mentioned to her about the green stuff in the console and that I couldn't figure out what it was. Her face turned red as she started giggling.

I hesitantly asked, "What's so funny? Do you know what the dried green stuff was?"

She laughingly explained, "Sunday when you rode to church with me, remember you kept trying to close the lid of the console as we were talking?

"Yes, I remember."

"Each time you hit the lid to close it, you turned over my smoothie that was in a plastic cup in the console. I didn't realize it then. I don't know why I forgot about it, because it was my breakfast, but we went on to church. The next day when I got into my car, I smelled the odor and remembered what had happened. I wasn't going to tell you, because I knew you'd feel bad about it. But, since you asked…I tried to clean it out, to no avail."

I stood in amazement. "Are you telling me, I did the green mess spill?"

"Yes," she replied, with a big grin on her face.

We looked at each other and started laughing so hard tears flowed down our cheeks.

I learned a valuable lesson that day. Never judge someone over smelly green goop in their car. Who knows? You may be the guilty one!

~ Gloria Spears

5
But He's Just a Puppy

My daughter, Brittany, has an affinity for animals. Her love affair with animals began as a young child when she was given stuffed animals by friends and family members for each birthday or for Christmas. She promptly gave each one a name.

When she was four years old she would line up, in alphabetical order, over 100 (that is not an exaggeration) stuffed animals. They sat shoulder to shoulder, single file, circling her bedroom floor.

One day my wife, Sandra, noticed that Brittany's stuffed animals were in a new order. She asked, "Why?"

Brittany whispered in her mother's ear. "I put them in the order I love them."

Sandra asked, "Britt, why are you whispering?"

She said, "I am whispering, Mommy, because I don't want to hurt any of their feelings."

During the next 20 years she has had eight dogs, five rabbits, seven turtles, numerous spiders, worms and ladybugs, a zillion hamsters, and 3,687 fish (I might be exaggerating a tiny bit).

She is still loving and collecting animals. The difference is, they are not stuffed, but living. She is a very busy lady but whenever she has a free moment she babysits other people's dogs, in addition to taking care of her own dog (Kirby), a newly adopted puppy (Mr. Finnegan), and her boyfriend's dog (Annie).

One weekend she had an out-of-town engagement and asked if Sandra and I would dog-sit all three dogs. We had the weekend free and a have a large fenced in back yard, so we agreed.

That was one of the worst decisions I have made in a long time.

Kirby could easily be nicknamed Mr. Wonderful. Annie never runs out of energy and is invariably the center of attention. Mr. Finnegan is whole different story.

One of my favorite pastimes is gardening. Through the years I have spent a great deal of effort making our backyard a place of beauty and solitude. In a matter of a few minutes our newest grandchild (with four legs and a tail) uprooted 10 plants, and rearranged 13 of my solar lights by pulling them out of the ground and depositing them in a densely wooded area on the back of our property. The plastic casings of my light fixtures were broken and the metal stems had teeth marks in them. Finn also found time to unplug the fountain in our fishpond, knock over three large potted plants and scatter the dirt from those pots. He pulled up and chewed much of a small decorative windmill.

All of this occurred in a record setting 64 minutes and 23 seconds!

By the time we discovered we could do without his contributions as a landscaper, we soon discovered he was just as skilled as an interior decorator. Upon coming inside, he promptly turned over two trashcans, then ate all of the other dogs' food. After removing the inner stuffing of a toy and overturning two water bowls, he pulled the cushions off the couch so he could take a well-deserved nap.

When I later brought all of that to the attention of my daughter, she apologized, smiled and said, "But Daddy, he's just a puppy."

I wish I had learned that excuse when I was going through my puppy days as a child. Like Mr. Finnegan, I did some pretty crazy things in a short amount of time.

Here are a few of my stupid moments:

For Adults Only: As a four-year-old child at a nearby lake, which had a depth of 250 feet, I floated on an inflatable raft to an "adult only" slide. Somehow, I avoided the lifeguard's attention, climbed a 15-foot ladder and slid down the long slide into the lake despite the fact that I did not know how to swim and was not wearing a life vest.

Dad, May I Borrow the Car? It was a hot summer day in July. My father was focused on cutting the grass and wasn't attentive to his eight-year-old son concerning the ice cream truck approaching our street. When I heard its melodious song, I asked, "May I get an ice cream cone, Dad? Please, Dad?" No response. Nothing. The truck rolled past and again I asked. "Dad, the ice cream man just missed us. May I borrow your car and catch him at the next street? I'll get you a Nutty Buddy and I'll get me a fudgsicle. Ok, Dad?" For the life of me I don't know why, but he said, "Yea, go ahead." Later on, I learned that he turned to my mother and asked, "Who's driving my car down the street?" Her response was, "I have no idea. But whoever it is, they are all over the road."

Cowboys & Indians: As a young boy I loved television westerns. Every Saturday morning I would rise before dawn, gobble down breakfast, and then put on my cowboy boots with silver spurs, my sheriff badge, and strap on my gun belt containing two six shooters loaded with caps. Like my television hero, I'd jump from a stagecoach to a wagon to a horse (our living room furniture) so I could get a better angle to shoot those dirty, rotten varmints. I learned to fire my six-shooter at the exact same time my hero fired his gun. Week after week, episode after episode, together we shot the bad guys.

One day, the unthinkable happened. One of the bad guys shot my hero. He lay on the ground as a bad man stood over him with a gun, ready to shoot him dead. I began to cry. My hero was going to breathe his last breath. I had to do something to save him! I rapidly fired several rounds of caps but none hit the mark. Realizing I had no more bullets I had to improvise. There was no time to waste!

There the bad man was standing over my hero with the hammer of his gun cocked. As quick as lightning I threw my six-shooter at him, hitting him in the head!

In those days televisions had glass screens. They operated on a system of tubes — sometimes as many as 20 — and fuses plugged into an electronic circuit board hidden behind the screen. First there was a loud explosion, then several smaller pops, sort of like fireworks on the fourth of July.

My parents ran into the room asking what had happened and why I was crying. "He shot my hero and I threw my pistol at the bad man's head to save him!"

They turned to the television set and saw my six-shooter lying inside the television on top of several sizzling tubes, surrounded by broken glass.

A week later, I learned my hero was not seriously hurt and was back in the saddle. As for me, it was several weeks before I was able to sit down on anything, if you know what I mean!

Somebody, Please Help Me: A memorable mishap, which could have been fatal, occurred when I was in fifth grade. A group of my neighborhood friends and I were playing soldiers at a nearby building site. It was in large housing development near some densely unoccupied woodland containing several large swamps.

Our favorite neighborhood event was a game of war. Each army would attack the enemy's camp as we hid behind piles of lumber while throwing grenades (water balloons) at the enemy troops. Our battles were always fun and physically challenging as we climbed over piles of dirt, gravel and sand.

One day I had a brilliant idea. The enemy never posted guards at the back of their fort. If I could circle their fort and enter by walking through the swamp, I could enter undetected and capture their flag.

It worked to perfection. Well, almost!

As I walked through the swamp I got stuck, really stuck. I tried to move but I could not. Then I realized I was not only stuck, I was sinking. I was caught in quicksand. I screamed and screamed and my friends finally found me and ran to get help. I had sunk up to my chest when a conglomerate of men from the construction crew, the fire department, and the police arrived to pull me to safety.

Needless to say, my soldier days came to an abrupt end as I was given a dishonorable discharge from my parents, the policemen, the firemen and the foreman of the building site.

Pirates of the Caribbean: Every summer I spent several weeks at my aunt and uncle's home in Weirton, West Virginia. They lived on a large piece of property, which was very narrow and several acres long. Their four-story house was conducive for all types of activities for a young boy with unlimited imagination. My favorite activity was playing pirates. I tied ropes from one banister to another. Some were taut for climbing while others were made for swinging. They allowed me to board another pirate ship in the midst of battle.

To this day I still don't know how it happened, but I pulled out a whole banister, several drainpipes and four two-story pieces of down spouting (Sounds a little like Mr. Finnegan, doesn't it?) while boarding an enemy pirate ship. My uncle was so mad that my pre-approved six-week summer vacation ended up lasting only four days. I was shipped home and never even received a bounty for keeping the harbor safe from pirates.

Have You Ever Watched *Shark Tank*? My wife and I enjoy watching Shark Tank where entrepreneurs present a new product or invention, hoping that someone on a panel of millionaires will be impressed and become a financial partner. That program did not exist when I was child. If it had, I would have thought I had a great product that would be a winner.

I was a seventh grader at that time. Two of my female cousins spent a lot of their summer sunbathing in hammocks. They would lie on one side and then turn to the other side.

I suggested they could save time and get tanned quicker and more evenly by following my instructions. I demonstrated my idea. I lay on my side and held a mirror at an angle on my stomach, and put another mirror on the ground to tan my back, allowing me to tan on both sides of my body at the same time.

Well, I am here to tell you it worked.

But what I had not counted on was a small technical glitch.

The intense heat from the mirror's reflection caught the hammock on fire.

Fortunately, no one got burned. My uncle decided not to send me home, but I did receive a good tongue-lashing and was prohibited from doing any more sunbathing the remainder of the summer.

My stories had some type of lesson in them that I decided to share with you. First, if you get your children or grandchildren a cute, cuddly puppy, I'd recommend you not name him Mr. Finnegan.

And when they do something really scary or dumb that makes you want to scream, count to ten, consider biting your lip before speaking, say a little prayer and remind yourself that each one is…just a little puppy.

~ Tommy Scott Gilmore, III

Men or Women?

With many errands to complete, I was in a hurry as I headed for the restroom in the shopping mall. Entering my destination, my first thought was: *This looks different than I remember it.* (I hadn't been to this mall for quite a while.) I hurried into the first stall and quickly sat down, in spite of the fact that the latch on the door didn't work properly. *They sure don't keep this place in good shape,* I thought.

I heard footsteps that were too heavy for a woman's, and suddenly I realized I was in the wrong restroom. Men's voices accompanied the footsteps and I wondered, *How am I going to get out of here without being seen? What if a man pulls open the door that isn't latched properly? Will the men see my shoes under the partition and know there's a woman in here?*

I seriously considered standing on the commode, but I was afraid my head would show over the top of the partition. I thought I might just stay there until the room cleared out. But more men kept coming in.

I finally decided my only option was to get out of there as fast as I could. When I reached the entrance, a man coming in got a funny look on his face and then looked up at the sign: MEN. The women's restroom was close by, so I quickly ducked in and stayed until I thought all the men who might have seen me had time to go on to do their shopping.

Needless to say, ever since that stupid (and embarrassing) happening, I always check the signs carefully before entering!

~ Elsie H. Brunk

ॐ 7 ॐ
Sweet Memories

After finishing the phone call with my husband, I glanced around at our much-loved-and-lived-in home.

Yikes! So much to do. My mother-in-law was coming to see her grandkids, Ken 13, Christopher 10, Adam 8 and the newest addition, Daniel 5 months.

The house wasn't dirty, but as my mother would have said, it was "strung and strewed." Baby items were everywhere. A playpen sat center stage, surrounded by stuffed toys, blankets, burp cloths, and just about anything else associated with having a new baby. All this alongside empty video game cases, the controls to the Nintendo and Sega, a pair of flip flops, dirty socks, empty chip bags, left-behind school books…and you get the picture of our busy home.

I made a list of things to do, starting with the never-ending piles of laundry. Boys and babies can generate quite the mountain of dirty clothes. The boys would take charge of their rooms and bathrooms and we would have our weekly Thursday Night Cleaning Party to handle the rest, including folding the laundry.

The day of their Grandma's arrival finally dawned. We settled her into the room shared by Christopher and Adam, who gladly gave it up for a chance to camp on Ken's floor for a week. It was time for Grandma to get down to some serious get acquainted time with her newest grandchild.

The days flew by in a flurry of the older boys' activities and sweet baby coos and kisses. Even the biggest boy, my husband Jim, got to spend some quality time with his mother.

One last meal was planned before Grandma's departure. Jim would grill steaks while the boys splashed in the pool. Grandma kept an eye on Daniel while I put together a salad, prepared potatoes for baking, and got out the ingredients for banana pudding, using my mother's recipe.

Since there was an extra mouth to feed, and this was one of all my boys' favorite desserts, I decided I needed to double the recipe. I made two large boxes of instant vanilla pudding rather than my usual one. I stirred into this a very large container of non-dairy whipped topping. The problem was, once I got all the vanilla wafers and bananas in the bowl and I began adding the pudding/topping mixture it wouldn't all fit into my pretty glass dish.

Not one to waste anything that could be reused or recycled, I dug out an old plastic butter container, its labels still on the top and the side. In went the extra pudding. I popped the container onto a shelf in the fridge. I finished off the pudding with a small container of the non-dairy topping, covered it with plastic wrap and slid my masterpiece into the fridge.

Soon, the steaks and the potatoes were done and we all gathered around the table to thank God for the food, for Grandma's time with us, and for traveling mercies as she headed home the next day.

Now, you need to know that I don't do fancy. I can count on one hand the number of times I have used my good china. Grandma's visit was no exception to the real me. I've always been one of those what-you-see-is-what-you-get kind of gals.

We began passing around the food, but I had forgotten to put the butter on the table. One of the boys jumped up and grabbed the container and handed it to Grandma.

She topped her potato with the butter, took a bite and said, "This tastes like . . . vanilla pudding." The look on her face said it all.

Needless to say, I was embarrassed, but it was so comical that we all got a good laugh out of the mistake. Obviously, the container with the pudding and not the butter had made its way to the table. Grandma scooped the pudding from her potato and slathered the real butter on it. We finished our meal and topped it off with the delicious banana pudding.

Grandma went home to be with Jesus in 2008, but we remember that day with lots of laughs. When we have baked potatoes in our home, we always ask, "Would you like some vanilla pudding with that?"

Thank you, Grandma, for all the years of love and for the fond, fond memories.

~ *Debra DuPree Williams*

Raisin Br-ants

I bowed my head and prayed, "Dear Lord, thank you for this beautiful day. Please bless this cereal to my body. Amen." I dipped my spoon into the bowl, and filled it full of crunchy flakes, plump raisins, and cold milk.

Ummm, ummm, I love Raisin Bran.

I took a few more bites, dropped my reading glasses from the top of my head to my nose, and opened my Bible. I read awhile, then dipped my spoon back into the bowl and brought it up to my mouth. Now my dentist has always told me that I have a small mouth, ahem, so I guess that's why I missed the opening, and ended up with milk dribbling down my chin. I turned from reading to clean my face, and noticed that my raisin bran looked a little strange.

Some of those raisins are really small.

I pushed my reading glasses up my nose, and leaned in closer.

Ugh! And they are swimming in the milk!

I spit and sputtered, and then glared at the surviving ants. But they didn't notice. They were too busy floating around in the milk, catching waves on raisins, and lounging on bran flakes. They were totally oblivious to the fact that a dollar pair of reading glasses had just saved them from being eaten alive. Ugh!

In Psalm 119, the psalmist asked God to open his eyes so he could see wonderful things in His law. But the psalmist wasn't referring to his natural eyesight that allowed him to read words and discover historical facts. The psalmist was asking God for supernatural illumination so he could understand deep, hidden, secret things in God's Word. He wanted to see spiritual things — God's glory and beauty and excellence.

Before I read my Bible, I pray and ask God to open my spiritual eyes so I might have discernment and commune with Him. And these days, I'm asking Him to help me remember my reading glasses — even when I'm eating cereal. I can still taste those raisin br-ants.

~ Susan Dollyhigh

❧ 9 ❧
Swimming with the Fishes

Many years ago, my son, Joe, had a favorite friend named Peewee. Peewee — the fish.

With cobalt blue and purple long-veiled tail, Peewee looked like no other sea creature my son had ever seen. His feathery fins seemed to flow in front, behind, and around him as he swam in the decorative bowl Joey bought with his three-dollar allowance.

"Peewee is a Japanese Fighter Fish." My six-year-old told everyone who would listen.

"He's pretty," I said, smiling at Joey and his dad.

My husband pointed to our larger 10-gallon tank where several aquatic species swam together. "I think Mom meant Peewee's a *pretty peculiar guy*."

True. Peewee wasn't an ordinary fish. His separate home proved it. Though he appeared to be the most beautiful Betta we had ever seen, he showed hostile territorial tendencies — or, he was just *mean*. — The opposite of an angelfish in almost every way.

"He's nice until he sees another fish," Joey said, while we tucked him into bed. "Then the little guy becomes a Siamese fighter. That's why he lives alone in a fish bowl built for one." But then, Joey pointed to the floor. "Peewee reminds me of the guy down there."

I looked around. "Down where?"

"You know, Mom…the real bad guy."

I tried not to laugh or, look at his dad. "Oh…*Him*." My eyes widened. I now understood Joey's concern for his pet acting like *the real bad guy*.

"Well," he continued, "if heaven is up there…"

We all looked up at the ceiling.

"And the other place is down there…"

All eyes went to the floor.

"I want to make sure Peewee doesn't think he's a shark, or a killer whale, like Sham-poo."

The next day, Joey's concern for Peewee escalated. He said he wanted to let Peewee swim in the big pond behind our house. He hoped the fighter would enjoy the exercise, and having more water to explore, he thought the fish would become friendly.

I remembered we recently told Joey about our upcoming move to a new home in two weeks. The thought of taking a dog, cat, a ten-gallon tank — and a smelly fish bowl to a new home worried me, but now with Joey's fears about heaven and you-know-where, I wanted to ease his concerns about his feisty friend's future.

We decided to take a walk down by the large pond early the following Saturday morning. Joey immediately said, "This place is perfect! Peewee wants to move into a bigger house too. He'll love this pond almost as much as you and Dad say I'll love my new room. Can we bring him here soon?"

I assured Joey Peewee shouldn't move to the big pond. I explained he could keep the fish in a bigger bowl in his new bedroom. "The Betta will be fine without fish friends."

Joey insisted he wanted Peewee to have a new adventure of his own.

"Are you sure?" I said, thinking Peewee would surely die after five minutes of swimming in the murky, bass-infested pond water.

Joey smiled and nodded.

We both ran home to tell his dad.

"Are you sure?" His dad said.

I stood behind Joey and shook my head, "No."

"Yes!" Joey said. And said. And said.

Before I knew it, I carefully scooped the fish into a Styrofoam coffee cup. Joey and I ran to the pond. Dad trailed behind us with the cup in hand.

Once at the edge of the pond, we all held hands and said a prayer for Peewee's safety. Joey took the cup from his dad and kneeled by the water's edge. He held it sideways to let the waters mingle. Soon Peewee ventured out into the open expanse. Cautious and slow, his colorful fins swayed in the still water. But then, Peewee turned and headed back toward shore — and his favorite friend.

"I don't think he wants to leave you," I said.

Joey looked at his dad. "We need to bring him out to the deeper water. Can Mom use my pool raft?"

I tried to object, but my husband bolted away. "I'll be right back."

Moments later, I wondered how I got into this mess. Paddling with one arm and a cup O' fish in the other hand, out to the middle of the pond I valiantly went. Barely balancing on the partially inflated plastic dingy and unaware my husband had also grabbed his camera when he went to get the long float, I quickly dumped Peewee out into the water and reached my arm back to set what was left of the dilapidated cup beside me. Now, with two arms paddling, I circled back toward shore…until…

"Waaaaaaait!" Little Joey's screech echoed through the air. "Peewee! Come back. You're my best friend."

I stopped dead. My mind raced. *Is he kidding? I think I'm sinking! Oh Lord what am I going to do? And what is that in his dad's hand?*

"Dennis! Are you taking pictures?" I barely said the words without gulping a mouth full of gross water.

"Try not to sink sweet pea. Don't hate me. I couldn't resist."

Joey looked at his dad and momentarily laughed with him. "Mom, Dad said you look kinda funny. But puh-lease. You have to save my Peewee before you yell at Dad for taking pictures from the shore!"

I tried to steer the float around one more time. Then, I saw a tiny ripple in the water next to me. "I see him! I can't believe this…Peewee followed me!"

The boys shouted, "Get him!"

Miraculously, Peewee swam right into the palm of my cupped hand. The rest of the rescue ride was a definite blur. On our walk back to the house my husband asked how I got the fighter back in the cup. To this day, I have no clue. It had to be divine intervention.

"You clung and swam, and laughed and flung." Joey said.

"You yelled and wailed all the way back to shore," Dennis chimed in, "and you almost totally deflated the kid's float." He winked at me. "Because that's what fun mom's do for their baby boys."

Later that afternoon I found out why this story eventually wound up on my all-time stupid moments list. Dennis came in from our backyard and set a tray of his delicious grilled chicken on the kitchen counter. After giving me a big bear hug, he said, "You did a wonderful, though crazy thing, out there today. I'd say you're almost ready to join the Coast Guard. You saved the day and more than that, I think you *really* may have saved Joey's best friend from *the bad guy*.

I expected him to look down at the floor, but he didn't.

"I'm happy Joey and Peewee had a grand adventure today. I'm even happier you're okay — and we're moving — especially since I spoke to our neighbor, Dave, while barbequing our dinner. He casually mentioned, 'You know, Mr. So-And-So down the street saw a four-foot gator in that pond yesterday.'"

~ Joann M. Claypoole

10
Computers, Too?

I'm well aware my computer knows more than I do, but sometimes it goes a mite too far. I contacted an interviewee about the article I was writing and needed clarification.

I wrote: "I wasn't sure where to put the Hinkling story. See below what I've written and put the Hinkling story where needed."

But this is what my computer sent in that email:

"I wasn't sure where to put the Hinkling story. See below what I've written and put the Honking story where needed."

Now, was that my computer's stupid moment? Or is that what's called, "getting edgy"?

~ Yvonne Lehman

11
Give Me a Thrill

Friends who knew me well used to hesitate before asking me to pray for them. This may seem bizarre, unless you know my history with prayers. You see, God tends to answer my prayers…just not exactly in the way I expect.

Before I realized I had a gift of praying for results, a friend and Bible study teacher asked me to pray that God's voice would be heard in class the following day. So, I prayed for God's voice, not hers, be heard. She showed up for class with laryngitis.

At a challenging time in my life when I had to make a decision about my job situation, I begged God to give me a sign as to whether I should stay or go. Less than an hour later, a neighbor banged on my door to wake me as flames engulfed my apartment. It burned to the ground. The next day, the transmission went out on my car. I no longer had anything to hold me to the job, or even the state. I resigned.

Of course, I can't forget the Christmas I met my husband. Feeling lonely and incomplete as a single woman, I prayed to meet someone before the end of the year. The purpose was to give me hope that I would eventually find a man to marry. It didn't have to be *him.*

At Christmas, a member of the church choir I directed invited me to her Christmas party. I didn't want to go. She would constantly ask if I was dating anyone, then give me tht look of pity when I answered in the negative. That grated on my nerves until I wanted to run from the room screaming or kill her. Since I didn't want to become a participant in a Christmas murder mystery, I attempted to find an excuse not to attend. Then, my best friend begged me to go with her to the party. I relented only because my friend's brother had just committed suicide and I thought she needed some social time. She needed me.

At the party, I met my future husband (thanks to the hostess!).

Now, this can be construed as a good answer or a bizarre and twisted answer to my prayer. I should have remembered the part where I said it didn't have to be my future husband, just a sign that there would be one. Eventually.

Enough said.

I have learned to think carefully before I pray. Unfortunately, I didn't learn this lesson in time to avoid the stupid prayer I wailed to the Lord one dreary day a few years ago.

Stormy skies reflected my mood that day. My life had become complicated by issues that were not my fault. Failing health and financial woes dragged me into a depressed stupor of playing the blame game and throwing a pity party that no one cared to attend. I needed sunshine. I settled for a drive in the mountains near Chattanooga, where I lived at the time. Clouds hung heavily all around me. That's when I pouted and turned an accusatory prayer to the Lord.

"Lord, why are you doing this to me? Please, fix it. I didn't ask for all of this negative stuff in my life. It's not my fault. I need something exciting in my life to get me out of this situation. Lord, give me a thrill."

Less than one minute later, as I meandered up Signal Mountain, with an expansive river on one side and the mountain on the other, a tree snapped, crashed on top of me, and trapped my van in a gnarled mass. Fear, trepidation, anxiety, and a touch of anger all exploded in my body.

Well, it was a thrill, I suppose. With effort, I maneuvered myself out of the crushed car and inspected the damage. Miraculously, the event left me without injury. The car was not so lucky.

I realized, as I sobbed and waved cars around me, that I had done it again. Why did I have to say *thrill*? Why hadn't I said *pleasant, happy experience*?

Stupid moments are expected by God. He uses whatever method we require to teach us important lessons. What I learned was not that I pray stupid prayers or that He answers my prayers in ways that can hurt me. I prayed as I did because I thought His love was not enough and that He was ignoring my needs. The answers He gave me proved the opposite. The day after my tree thrill, I learned of a couple who had experienced the same thing. Unfortunately, they didn't survive their tree. Even though I could have died just as easily in the fire or the tree experience, God protected me. He had a purpose for me.

So, if you want some excitement in your life, ask me to pray for you. If you need a specific prayer answered, write it down in clear, concise language that leaves no room for surprises, and I will pray that for you.

Anybody need a thrill today?

~ Karen Nolan Bell

ॐ 12 ॐ
A Sordid Sunday Afternoon

Five or six years ago, my wife and I drove from Richmond, Virginia, to the mountains of western North Carolina for the first annual Novelist Retreat. While the drive is a reasonable length — six or seven hours including meals and rest stops — we'd left home early that day and were thoroughly worn out by the time we arrived at the Lifeway Ridgecrest Conference Center near Black Mountain. We could hardly wait to sack out for a while before getting ready for the evening meal.

Check-in seemed to take forever, but we were finally on our way up the hill to the Mountain Laurel Inn. We grabbed a cart at the entrance to the building and returned to the car for our stuff. We don't travel light. We finally headed to our room, rescuing small items as they fell off the cart.

When we unlocked the door, a fruit basket on the table caught our immediate attention. As often as we'd been to Ridgecrest before, we'd never enjoyed an amenity like that. We unwrapped it. The note read, "Thanks Yvonne" — no comma.

Ah? The conference director was giving conferees fruit baskets in appreciation for our taking a chance on the new conference? How generous! Although we weren't hungry at the moment, we did polish off the grapes before unloading and returning the cart. Then, as we normally do when staying somewhere longer than overnight, we unpacked and put everything away.

Only then did we discover that our room was different from the Mountain Laurel rooms we'd stayed in before. We had more space. Lots more.

Huh? They'd put us in a suite? Nice!

We'd never realized Mountain Laurel had suites, and we certainly hadn't paid for one. Perhaps we should've been more suspicious, but we concluded that maybe a larger conference was taking place at the same time as ours and Ridgecrest had run out of regular rooms and had to give us the suite out of necessity — at the price of a regular room.

We were too tired to question our unexpected blessing. So we pulled the spread back, took off our shoes — we were fully clothed otherwise — and lay down. Before long, we were both snoozing.

We'd barely fallen asleep when a strange noise woke us up. Someone was unlocking our door. Housekeeping? No, couldn't be. The room — the suite — was completely ready when we got there. Nothing more needed to be done.

But somebody was about to come through the door, and I couldn't imagine that any of the bears living in the nearby woods had learned to use a key card. Or that the intruder was Goldilocks.

No. Not Goldilocks, but a blonde all right.

Conference director Yvonne Lehman looked at us and we looked at her. What in the world was she doing barging into our suite unannounced — and with her own key?

After a few minutes of talking and laughing over our improbable situation, I discovered I'd been asking myself the wrong question. The right one was, *What in the world are we doing in Yvonne's suite*?

With the confidence of an experienced conference director, she called the front desk and explained the situation. Someone showed up moments later with a new key for us — for a different room. One that looked disappointingly similar to all the other rooms in Mountain Laurel that weren't suites.

We couldn't complain, though. We liked Mountain Laurel, and — after all — we got what we'd paid for. Finally.

Ever since that crazy afternoon, Yvonne and I have had more fun over that stupid moment — thank goodness it wasn't her fault or ours — and I always greet her at conferences with a hearty, "Hello, roomie." Preferably with other people nearby, people who can't help overhearing and wondering what in the world I'm talking about.

At this year's Novelist Retreat, however, Yvonne revealed our "sordid" story publicly to the delight of the other conferees. I wish I could make a stupid moment sound as hilarious as she did, but her southern drawl is more convincing and she's been an author and story teller a lot longer than I have.

My day will come, though.

~ *Roger E. Bruner*

If a matter is not serious enough to pray about it,
then it is not serious enough to worry about.
And if it is serious enough to pray about,
and we have prayed about it,
then there is no need to worry about it.
James E. Bibbons

13

From 14-Karat Mind to the Mind of Christ

After making my entrance into the hotel ballroom to attend a fashion show with several friends, I searched the tables to find my name card. There was Eleanor, motioning to me and patting a seat. "Vicki, so glad to see you. Sit next to me."

What an honor. Eleanor was the classiest lady I'd ever met. She was gracious, loving, thoughtful, and a mentor during my young adult years. I was delighted to sit next to her. She always sported a look of polish and perfection. Never had I seen a mascara smudge beneath her beautiful eyes. Her clothes, with never a wrinkle in a linen skirt, were likely purchased in New York, San Francisco, London, Dallas, or Atlanta. Bedecked with jewelry — she always wore complete sets — she was the epitome of fashion.

I was still waiting to get a ruby necklace that would match my ring. After that addition, perhaps I'd put a ruby bracelet on my wish list. Then maybe I'd try to finish out a sapphire set. Wouldn't emeralds be nice? And pearls! Every Southern girl had to have a bracelet to match her pearl necklace and earrings. Especially one with diamonds. Maybe one day.

Then I remembered. "A big congratulations to you, Miss Eleanor, for making the Ten Best Dressed Women list. I only dream of making that list — ha-ha," I said. "Though it will take a lot of work and will be daunting, I'll have to try to follow in your footsteps."

Always humble, the virtuous and charitable woman beside me said, "Oh, Vicki, being on that list and having my name in the newspaper has its downside. Now, every time I step out of my house, I'm afraid not to dress to perfection for fear someone will say, 'How in the world did she ever make that list?' It's an honor, but truly, I don't like the scrutiny."

Surprised at this candid confession, I replied, "I never thought about it that way. Maybe you're right. Making the list sort of puts you under a magnifying glass or, it's similar to living in a glass house. Perhaps I don't want to be on that list! I'm usually wearing blue jeans and flannel shirts. I refuse to dress up to go to the grocery store or the feed store. Some days I haul hay in the trunk of my car!"

"Exactly what I'm talking about," said Eleanor.

Hmmm. Other friends began to seat themselves next to us, and the fashion show commenced. While watching beautiful, thin models glide down the runway I began thinking more about what Eleanor had said. Her words were pearls of wisdom. I could imagine the critics coming out in droves to see if an honored one could hold her place on the high pedestal once she made the Best Dressed list.

I could almost hear them saying things about me like, "That outfit sure makes her look chunky."

"Someone as short as she, should avoid horizontal stripes. What was she thinking?"

"Why did she ever, in her wildest dreams, think she could rock the color orange? Disaster the minute she stepped off the front step."

"Her hair is a mess today. Wonder who told her she could sport a pony tail. Makes her look so horsey and downright long in the tooth."

I could hardly eat the salad placed in front of me for thinking about mucking out a barn, breaking a sweat and getting my jeans filthy. And that mission trip I'd gone on to Jamaica — the one where I had to hike a mile and a half down a mountain to get to church in hot, humid weather, with my hair plastered to my damp scalp. Then I'd hiked back up to the mission listening to the sounds of bleating goats, crowing roosters, and thinking about the moaning men who'd gotten into machete fights the night before. No glamorous moments there.

Thank the Lord there had been no photographers around to record those unflattering snapshots of me looking like a wilted magnolia blossom! Let's just call it like it was…I'd been a sweaty mess.

I sighed as I waited for the chicken entrée to be set before me and watched the next pouty model purse her lips before making a well-heeled turn back to the dressing room and a fast change. I kept dwelling on Eleanor's words and my all around casual life in general. There were certainly no silk dresses or fancy jewelry on that Caribbean trip.

Plain and simple, I enjoyed letting my hair down. A lot. I'd much rather be roasting hot dogs over an open fire down at the pond with my children than worrying if the linen skirt I wore was beginning to look like a limp dishrag.

As I watched to see what icon of fashion finesse would next appear on the runway, I wondered if Eleanor had ever heard of Jesus Christ. Though she was Jewish, was she devout? Should I approach the subject? No. Best not go there. Wouldn't want to offend her. I'd let God handle that subject.

A couple of years passed and I was notified of Eleanor's death. I arrived late at the synagogue to pay my last respects; almost everyone else had already gone. A sad feeling fell over me like a final curtain made of wet sagging velvet. There was more meaning behind my tears and I knew it. The loss was more than losing a treasured friend. I couldn't stop crying for this woman. Yet I couldn't quite explain my emotions to her family.

Perhaps the copious tears had to do with my never broaching the subject of the Messiah with her. That he'd already come and he'd died for her. I wondered if anyone had told her about Jesus before she breathed her last. I'd had a "religious" decision to make when it came to Eleanor and I'd chosen not to broach the subject of Jesus.

Many years passed before I had to make a similar "religious" decision — speak up about Christ or stay silent. I recalled the verse from Matthew 10:33: **"Whoever denies me before men, I will also deny him before my Father who is in heaven."**

I certainly didn't want to deny Christ, but I didn't want to offend anyone either. *Lord, there are better equipped people to share the Gospel with those of other faiths. Please send someone else.*

When a friend lost her son in a tragic death by suicide from a river's bridge, I had to make a choice. I could tell this grieving woman of the Hindu faith about the only Son of God who could heal her emotional wounds and take a chance I might offend her…or I could keep silent. *Lord, help me here*, I cried out. *This woman is in agony and you know I'm not good at this witnessing to people about my own faith much less to those of other faiths. What should I do?*

Six months after the death of her son and after much prayer, I called and invited her to dinner during the Christmas holidays. Before the appointed time, I searched for a book about Jesus that I could wrap and give her as a Christmas present.

When the evening arrived, I gathered up this precious woman — still in grief knee-deep and mire-mixed with anger because of the loss of her only son — and whisked her off to try to help ease her battle-scarred mind.

"I've never been out to dinner without my family," shared my friend. Shocked at this revelation from a very modern and highly-trained woman who held an important job in a professional field, I listened as she poured out her story. A woman from her country was expected to marry someone of her parents' choosing. There were never any girls-night-out with women friends. Ours was her first. The tragedy of losing her son had rocked her world.

After an excellent dinner and much-needed girl-talk, on the way home I determined I would have no regrets concerning my cherished friend of the Hindu faith like the regrets I had with Eleanor, my Jewish friend. Somehow, I would gather the courage to mention Jesus to the woman in the seat next to me, even though her family did not celebrate Christmas and the birth of Christ.

While sitting in the car at her home, I gave her the gift. As she unwrapped the book, I explained that the reading material was about Jesus, the only Son of God, the one who claimed so many years ago, "I am the way, the truth, and the life, and no one comes to the Father except through me." Perhaps Jesus would heal her hurts like he'd healed so many of mine if she gave him a chance and called on him to help her.

My dear friend immediately began to share about her 30,000 gods. I was semi-literate about her 30,000 gods and the Hindu belief that humans were reincarnated and kept coming back to relive life on earth until they "got it right" or something along those lines.

Frankly, I stopped studying about Eastern religions when I shuddered to think I could come back as a rat, which was so repulsive to me that I was even more convinced Jesus was the real deal, though I'd never had a doubt that Jesus was the only way, and who he claimed to be.

When my friend finished trying to enlighten me, however, I thanked her for sharing, and we hugged goodbye.

On the way home, I prayed, "Lord, I did what I felt you wanted me to do.

I have introduced my friend, the wonderful person our Father created, to you and I place her salvation solely in your hands and pray the Holy Spirit will eventually stir her heart so she will come to know you and the Father like I know you."

I'm still waiting for the living-happily-ever-after story ending. That phone call — the one where my friend says, "I've found Jesus and have made him my Lord and Savior so I will live eternally!" So far, I haven't heard those words from her. I know, however, that all is in God's timing and my prayers are being heard. But there is one good thing that has come from my sharing about the Messiah to those of different faiths. I no longer have a 14-karat mind. I quickly came to the realization that Jesus is right, my earthly treasures can't go to heaven with me. There are more important things to do on earth than polishing silver and gold and adding to collections. I'm working every day to be more Christ-like, striving to have a mind like Christ because I want no more regrets. And I'm going to repeat this verse often: Who has known the mind of the Lord, that he may instruct him? But we have the mind of Christ. (1 Corinthians 2:16)

And besides, the walls of the New Jerusalem — the heavenly city where I'll be living while not hanging out in the heavenly barn — are built on foundations made of sapphires and every kind of jewel including emeralds and the streets are paved with gold. I will have no need for matching jewelry sets or silk dresses or unwrinkled linen. I'll be arrayed wearing garments of salvation and robes of righteousness.

Who could ask for more?

- Vicki H. Moss

~ 14 ~
Oops!

In my defense, planning has never been my specialty.

Our son Bobby wanted to celebrate his fifth birthday with a party at the roller skating rink. Perfect. I'd merely show up with a few decorations and a cake. Then I'd relax while raking in the praise for a perfect party.

Bobby rose early on his birthday, ready to roll. Arriving at the rink, he led the way, his little arms overloaded with decorations. I followed, balancing his birthday cake and presents while pushing his sister, Brittany, in the stroller. A broad smile broke across Bobby's face as he stepped through the door, greeted by loud music and colorful lights bouncing across the walls and the hardwood floor.

We claimed a table, set out the few party decorations, and rented skates. There was nothing left to do but lace on the skates and wait for his friends to arrive.

We laced and waited. And waited. And waited.

Bobby's smile began to fade, Brittany began to squirm, and I stared at the entrance willing his friends to appear. They didn't.

Needing a distraction, I said, "Let's go ahead and start skating."

Brittany squealed with delight as I pushed her in the stroller. Bobby laughed as he teetered in his skates, ever on the brink of a wipe out. We both shot occasional glances towards the entrance.

Twenty minutes crept by. No guests.

"When are my friends going to get here?" Bobby asked.

"They'll be here soon," I said, feigning cheerful. *I know it's hard to be on time while schlepping kids around, but surely one of my friends could've gotten their child here on time.*

More time passed. Bobby's voice dripped with sadness. "Mommy, are my friends not going to come to my party?"

I tried to hide my simmering anger with a feeble smile. *How could they do this to Bobby on his birthday?*

And then it hit me. *I sent out invitations, right?*

Like a foghorn blaring through a dense mist, reality broke through and punched me square in the gut. *No one was coming to Bobby's birthday party because I'd never invited anyone.*

Tears spilled from Bobby's eyes and his lower lip quivered as I confessed to what I'd *not* done.

"No one's coming to my party?" he said.

I shook my head in shame. *What kind of mother forgets to invite anyone to her son's birthday party? Who plans a party and forgets the guests?* I pushed aside my humiliation, grabbed my cellphone, and placed frantic calls to my friends. I reached two. Only one could come.

In super-hero timing, Traci flew through the door and salvaged the party. Bobby beamed as Traci appeared not only with her son in tow, but with a large gift as well. I suspected her son was missing a toy from his closet.

This disastrous moment spotlighted what I'd too often regarded as my stellar qualifications for *Scum Mother of the Year*. As Bobby and his sole guest rolled around the rink laughing, I had a choice to make. I could sink into despair over my imperfections, or I could sink into the peaceful comfort of grace — both God's grace and the grace my young son had been extended to me. I could thrash myself for my repeated failings, or I could laugh. I chose grace. I chose to laugh. Traci laughed, too, and forbade me from planning any more parties on my own.

Since that birthday debacle, my planning skills haven't improved much. I continue to provide ample opportunities for my loved ones to laugh and practice forgiveness skills. Their abundant grace has covered a mountain of my *Oops!*

God's amazing grace has covered it all.

Whew!

~ Jean Wilund

15
Don't Ask!

My daughter, son-in-law, and 16-year-old grandson, Simon, and I went out to dinner. Simon opened doors and held them for us. Favorably impressed and wanting him to know I particularly noticed, I jested, "Do you hold the doors open for me because I'm old, or a female?"

"Both."

Talk about asking a bright boy a stupid question!

Fortunately, he grinned and had a twinkle in his eye.

~ Yvonne Lehman

16
The Library Book

It was late when we returned to the hotel from a family wedding. The kids changed and crawled into bed. David and I lay down next to them.

"Sorry, Sweetie," I said, "as tired as I feel, I don't think I can sleep. I'll read my library book for a while."

"That's fine, Babe. I'm sure the light won't bother the kids. In fact, I think they're out."

Before I read half a page, my eyes started to droop and the words became blurred. I quietly put my book inside the night stand and turned off the light.

Crash, pop, crack, screech. My ears ached with the magnitude of the loudest noises I'd ever heard. I tried to raise my hands to cover my ears, but they were tangled in my sheets.

My body swung from one side of the bed to the other. I felt like a rag doll in the hand of an angry toddler. I tried to yell, but the horrendous clatter was too much.

I waited.

My dry mouth choked out, "What…is…going…on?"

David blared, "Don't move. It's an earthquake. Just stay where you are."

"Dad," Joshua shouted, "it's so loud and dark!"

"I know, Joshua, just hang on to Gretchen!"

The thunderous sound of the building breaking slowly subsided. A tomb-like silence descended on the hotel. I wasn't sure which was more alarming, the deafening noise or the lack of it.

There was movement on the bed. "David, what are you doing?"

"I'm going to turn the lights on."

"Ouch!"

"What's wrong? Are you okay?"

"Yea, I hit my leg on something on the floor."

"The lights are out." A strange green glow suddenly lit up around David. "At least the light on my watch should help. I see what I hit my shin on."

I crawled over to the edge of the bed. The television that had been bolted on the dresser the night before lay broken in pieces.

"You guys stay here," he said. "I'm going to run to the van to get the flashlight."

I crawled over to the other bed, "You guys okay?"

"Just great, Mom, but could you tell Gretchen that she can let go of me now?"

"I was making sure you didn't fall," Gretchen told him. "Just because you're 14 and I'm 12, I can still save you."

"Yeah, right, Sis."

Suddenly the bed tilted sideways and we grabbed each other. At that moment no one seemed to care who held whom.

As the aftershock settled, David ran in with the flashlight. Our hands flew up to shield our eyes, "Hey, Dad, would you mind dropping that light a little lower. I'd like to make it out of here with my sight intact."

"Wow," David retorted, "just 12 and you're already demanding."

We all laughed.

David let the light filter around the room. Cracks zigzagged along the walls. Plaster littered the floor. The light shone into the bathroom. Water dripped from the toilet and faucet. My heart started to pound as I came face to face with the destruction. It could have been so much worse.

We hurriedly dressed, before a couple of mild aftershocks threw us off balance.

I knew the next words out of my mouth would sound crazy. "David, I think we should probably check out."

"You don't mean like go down to the office and turn our keys in and get a receipt, do you? I really don't think anyone is going to be sitting in that office just waiting for people to turn in their keys."

"I know, I know, but I would feel better if we tried. It doesn't seem right to just leave."

He put his head down and I saw his chest heave a sigh. He nodded.

We left the kids in the room with a promise to be right back. We didn't know if it was safer inside or out.

I wrapped my arm around David as we made our way to the office. We both stood and stared through the open door. Our jaws dropped to our chest. Computers lay smashed on the floor. Papers covered the counters and a lot of cash lay on the floor. I looked around and found a white table cloth crumpled in the corner. I placed it over the money. Somewhere in my brain I decided if no one could see it, it wouldn't get stolen. I put our keys in a drawer I found on the floor.

"Okay, we can go now. I feel better," David stared at me blankly.

"I know, it was dumb, but thanks for indulging me."

We hurried back to our room, grabbed the suitcases, the kids, and made our way to the van.

The kids scrambled into their seats and I climbed in the front. I froze. "David, we can't leave yet."

"Dianna, what do you mean? We already checked out. What else could possibly be wrong? We need to get out of here."

"No, I left my library book in the room and I have to get it. I'll get fined if I don't return it on time and I don't want to pay for it. It's really big!"

Even as the words left my mouth, I knew I was being irrational again, but I felt compelled to get that book.

David peered over the backseat at the kids. They both shrugged in confusion. "Kids, we'll be right back."

We returned to our room and, of course, being the conscientious patron, I had locked our door as we left. You never knew when a gang of burglars were headed our way to rob our hotel just after a major earthquake. I just had to take those keys back. What was I thinking?

I looked over at David with a half-hearted smile. "Sorry."

Without a moment's hesitation, David lifted his leg and kicked the door. It cracked. He lifted his foot again. The second kick shattered the middle of the door, but now his leg was stuck inside our room.

As he worked to dislodge his leg from the door, I thought it best to look away. A bout of the giggles would not go over well. I scanned the area to see if anyone had seen us. I was an accessory. I had never done anything illegal before. Well…except on my wedding night when I drank a sip of champagne while I was underage. Really, Dianna, where did that thought come from? What is so darn important about a library book? Just get the book and go. I felt exasperated with myself.

David dislodged his leg after much grumbling and shoved the door open. I grabbed my book and we ran back to the van.

A day after we arrived in Arizona, we watched a news report on the earthquake. It happened in Northridge, California, only eight miles from our hotel — 6.8 on the Richter scale. The news report mentioned the freeway we took to leave California was the only one open. All the others were damaged. Our guardian angels had been busy.

Two days later I proudly walked into my public library and set the library book on the counter. I smiled with the joy of my accomplishment and I walked away with my head held high.

~ Dianna Beamis Good

17
Toilet Tissue Tale

I'm not a big fan of the mall; I only go a few times throughout the year. Most of my visits are during the holiday season. A trip to the mall is an adventure in itself. People seem to have no cares in the world. Everyone seems to be whistling a happy tune. I want to dash in and get out. I don't care for the crowds and the prices. If you ask anybody about me, they would know that I'm a thrifty shopper.

Have you ever notice where the restrooms are located in the malls, especially in older malls? They are located in secluded areas. You have to travel down back end corridors to find them. Just the thought of where they are is creepy. I don't like walking alone down a long corridor. Nothing bad has ever happened to me, but I have heard horrible stories. I don't want to be a statistic.

One particular day while at the mall, I had to potty. It seemed that I traveled two miles to get there. I was thinking if I really had to go severely, I would never make it. This could be an embarrassing moment.

The mall was full of the weekend crowd. People seem to be everywhere buying and shopping. I finally arrive to the secluded restrooms. I made a quick dash in and out. I did take the time to wash my hands. I headed out relieved that this adventure was over.

Well…so I thought.

I felt a hungry urge come upon me, so I headed toward the concourse of the mall, to find the food court area. I walked around until I found the food vendor, from where I wanted to eat.

While standing in line, a nice lady approached me and said, "You have something hanging out."

I looked back and discovered I had a toilet tissue tail. I was so embarrassed.

I'm so thankful this most embarrassing incident happened a long time ago. If it occurred today, I would probably be a viral YouTube sensation.

~ *Audrey Tyler*

18
Leaders Gone Wild

As a young couple, my husband and I were always the first to volunteer at church. The task really didn't matter, whether it was setting up the fellowship hall for an event or cleaning up the mess after the event. We just loved being a part of our church family and helping however we could.

"I got a call from Pastor Jerry today," my husband mentioned one evening. "He would like us to consider leadership in the young married adult ministry."

I looked at him with interest, "Really? What do you think?"

"I like the idea, but let's pray about it."

We accepted the call to leadership, eagerly jumping in to immerse ourselves in this grand adventure we believed the Lord was calling us into. We became part of a leadership team that consisted of three other couples.

The church had four small groups that met each month for Bible study and prayer. Once a quarter the four groups would get together for an outing or a special time of worship. There was an anointing in these gatherings. My husband and I grew spiritually beyond what we could have imagined. I can't say for sure when our leadership teams started down that dark road of clandestine, out-of-line behavior, but once it began, it consumed us.

Outside our ministry duties, we were getting together as friends. We would have barbecues, go to the beach, or the ladies would go for coffee and shopping. Although we loved each other, a growing competitive spirit began to develop.

"Yep, I broke your home run record on Thursday," one would say, "guess you're getting a little too old for this game."

"Well, we had 30 people in our last study, I heard you had…how many, seven?"

I suppose it started innocently enough — the guys trying to outdo each other at golf or softball, who had more people attending their group — mostly having fun picking at each other. But the night of the first yard rolling (aka tp-ing and house wrapping, depending on what part of the country you're from) started our long, nefarious fall from grace.

My husband and I were not the first targets, nor did we take part in that first "crime." But once word got out, we excitedly joined in the devious behavior and were part of the second crime. Pandora's box had been opened.

Our "payback" took yard-rolling to a whole new level. We covered the yard, the bushes, and the trees — palm trees mind you, no easy task. Not holding back, we moved on to our next target the same night. Our group had been studying Moses and the Jewish exodus from Egypt. We decided to give a warning to others who may be tempted to carry out payback of their own, so we took a verse from Exodus 12 and tweaked it a little: The toilet paper shall be a sign for you on the houses where you live; and when we see the toilet paper we will pass over you, and no calamity will befall you to destroy you when we strike the land of Ft. Lauderdale.

We posted the sign with our proclamation on the door we had marked for warning, and secured some toilet paper over the top of the doorframe. We were having such fun and laughed all the way to the Waffle House for our celebratory midnight breakfast.

At the time, I was administrative assistant to our music minister and privy to all the office talk about what was going on in the young adults group.

"It's just a little silliness," I remember our sweet, old custodian saying.

"It's outright sinful!" our receptionist scolded.

I kept quite, but thought it was just some fun between friends. However, it began to snowball. The yard rolling continued until that got boring, so we went to sticking plastic forks all over front yards. From there we added paper plates, sticking them in the ground with the forks. I feared things might be getting out of hand when some took to dumping lawn clippings on front porches. The buzz in the church office had started to elevate, and there was talk that something would have to be done.

I must confess that my husband and I were there on the fateful night that brought our "innocent" fun crashing to an end. The incident was indeed horrific — wet gummy worms thrown all over a sliding glass door. It was a nasty mess. We were actually caught that night as the gummy worms made a slight plopping sound against the glass. We ran like crazy. Once we had regrouped in the van, we knew it had gone too far, so back we went to clean up the sticky chaos we had created.

"The gossip at church is growing." I acknowledged.

"Well, after all we are *leaders*!" my husband responded a bit sarcastically.

That night the group agreed it had to stop. It was finished, kaput, over… or so we thought.

When crimes are committed, there must be punishment.

Our sentencing came quickly, without a trial, on the following Sunday morning. Our pastor called us out from the pulpit. Though he did not call us by name, or call witnesses, or even give a summary of evidence, he did give closing arguments. We were reprimanded, humiliated, and ashamed. Being a kindhearted pastor, his verdict was given in love, with a touch of humor. "Fun though these pranks may be, the shenanigans will stop and you will return to your ministry and be the leaders you have been called to be."

We look back and laugh at our youthful indiscretions, knowing our antics were all in fun. From this chapter in our ministry we gleaned a valuable lesson about stopping things before they get out of hand, and a wise, Godly pastor taught us how to lead with love, forgiveness…and ok, maybe a *little* fun!

~ Janet Bryant Campbell

19
Does This Tube Make My Butt Look Big?

Entertaining people is something I enjoy doing. However, my intentions were not to entertain, but educate my friend.

We had gone to spend the weekend at a camp at Weeki Wachee Springs, Florida. The parents of a friend of mine ran the camp and would allow us to come up for the weekend during the off season. We loved to take advantage of the cabins and river fun.

Shelia and her daughter, me with my two daughters were off for a fun weekend.

Our agenda included tubing down the river. So off we went to see Bob for our tubes. Now, I am not a small woman. Having said that, it appears I had an expanded concept of my derriere.

After everyone else had picked out their tubes, my turn came. I told Bob I wanted the biggest tube he had, so he picked one out and filled it with air. Looking at the tube I was thinking *are you kidding me, that hole will not fit around my butt.*

Shaking my head back and forth, while looking from the tube to Bob, I murmured, "Bigger?"

He chuckled. "I don't think we need to go bigger."

"Oh yes we do," I insisted.

"Ok, I'll be right back." He turned and walked to the back of the shed.

Out he came with the biggest tube I had ever seen. He started the compressor and proceeded to fill the tube.

Staring at the tube as it grew larger and larger, my smile grew with it.

"Yes, this is the tube for me."

Bob just shook his head and starting laughing.

Ready for the river, we gathered our gear and headed off down the path toward our adventure.

What a sight to see, three young girls with their swimsuits on, carrying their tubes and towels. One mom around five feet tall, a little full around the middle, and me, the giant of the group at five feet nine inches.

Once we were in the knee-deep waters it was time to get everyone into their tubes. Sheila's height was making it difficult for her to get into her tube. So being the helpful educator that I am, I confidently told her to watch me do it.

I backed up against my humongous tube, then placed my hands on each side of it. I took the leap backwards, attempting to place my rear in the center of the tube, expecting the hole in the tube to wrap its rubber self around my backside like a tight rubber band. To my surprise, my body folded itself in half, with my toes and hands sticking up into the air. I slid right through that tube and hit the bottom of the riverbed.

Shocked and amazed, I surfaced. Wiping the water from my face I turned to face my friend and found her doubled up with laughter. I can only imagine what a funny scene I had created.

My laughter filled the river bank as I looked around for the tube and found it headed down the river without me in it. As I took in the scene and tried to comprehend what had exactly happened I turned toward the river bank. To my surprise there were about 10 people standing there watching me. I could tell they were trying not to laugh but I knew what they had witnessed had been funny.

I looked at them, smiled, bowed, and waved. "I know it was funny," I shouted. "Go ahead and laugh."

That was one of my best stupid moments.

But following that embarrassment was the jubilation that, no, my behind was not as large as I had envisioned!

~ Lillian Humphries

✧ 20 ✧
I'm Melting

Instilling Honesty and Integrity in Your Children

My five-year-old son had developed a habit of lying, and I was determined to stop it. After numerous attempts at spanking, I wanted a creative approach.

Finally, I devised my plan. One year earlier, Hendrix had become interested in Star Wars. One of his treasured possessions was my old collection of action figures.

I decided that when he lied, he needed to feel regret in an area that mattered to him. So, I created a new rule: He lost one action figure for every lie. One evening I initiated what I thought was the perfect tactic of creative discipline. Hendrix told a lie, and I instructed him to bring me one Star Wars man and meet me in the kitchen. He listened to my speech about the destructive nature of lies. Then, I proceeded to heat up the frying pan. I told my son that what I was about to do to his action figure illustrates the horrible effects of lies. Hendrix and I watched Han Solo slowly melt away until only a puddle of oozing plastic goo remained.

I thought, *What a great plan. The little guy will remember this forever. This may break the pattern of lies tonight. James Dobson should feature this idea in one of his books.* I looked up at Hendrix, expecting him to break into uncontrollable sobs, wailing, "Daddy, I will never lie again! I've learned my lesson!"

Instead, Hendrix, who had not taken his eyes off of the frying pan, flashed his bright smile and excitedly asked, "Can we do another one, Daddy?"

So much for creative discipline.

Children catch many of life's values as we model them — not as we plan the perfect lesson. Several years after the Han Solo melting, our family experienced an object lesson in integrity and truth-telling.

Vacationing in Pigeon Forge, we ate supper at one of the infamous pancake houses. After eating, we left the dining room and waited to pay for several minutes in the large, separate, unattended foyer and gift shop. My children looked at pocket knives. Finally, a manager entered, apologizing for the delay. "Thank you for your honesty," he said." You have no idea how many people in your situation just leave the store and do not pay."

Then, seeing Hendrix looking at the pocket knife, he said, "Please, take the pocket knife at no charge. That is my way of saying thank you for being honest."

Today, my family still has that knife with "Pigeon Forge" carved on its side. And occasionally, one of the children will say, "That is the knife the man gave us because we were honest." That small knife reminds us of the importance of integrity.

Here are practical ways to instill integrity:

Explain what integrity means.

Teach children that integrity means to be the same on the inside as you claim to be on the outside. The word is associated with the testing of metals. Some rings are gold-plated. Others are solid gold all the way through. God wants us to be the real deal.

Read and memorize key verses.

During mealtimes or family devotions, review Bible texts about the importance of truth-telling. Some examples are Proverbs 12:19, Ephesians 4:15 & 25, John 8:44, John 14:6.

Read stories about people of integrity.

As a family, read or listen to radio theater stories of people with integrity (Gladys Aylward, Corrie ten Boom, and George Müller). Then discuss lessons from their lives. Also recommended are William Bennett's *The Children's Book of Virtues* and *The Children's Book of Heroes*.

Jesus is in the room.

We try to teach our children that we always live in God's presence. At times we will say, "I need you to answer me with Jesus standing in the room with us."

Sour tongue.

When children do lie, take a small dab of vinegar and put it on their tongue. We call this "sour tongue." The awful taste reminds them of how lies taste to God.

Model honesty and integrity.

No better training exists than Dad and Mom living lives worth replicating before their children. Those little ones see us day in and day out. Remember, they catch what we do and say — and what we don't say.

May our children find us to be people of integrity — the real deal — just like the gold rings that are solid all the way through.

- Dr. Rhett H. Wilson, Sr.

~ 21 ~
Prepared for Presentation

I was on a team that had traveled to South Africa to offer support to church staff. My job was to lead the conference, present ideas and methods to church workers regarding preschoolers in church.

I had worked at Ridgecrest Conference Center in North Carolina and in Baptist churches for several years. However, this was the first time I was to lead and present in that kind of conference setting. Most of the South African leaders were older than I, age 24, but were new to church ministry.

Despite being nervous, I was completely prepared with handouts and supplies we had organized. My confidence grew as all seemed to be going well. Participation was good, and people were happy and smiling throughout my presentation.

While meeting the workers and shaking hands as conferees left, I noticed something strange. Then I realized my white linen coat was inside out, pockets and all.

No one had mentioned it, but maybe some of those wide smiles were a hint. Throughout the day, either they had been very gracious or figured that was the American style. As soon as courtesy allowed, I went around the corner, embarrassed for sure, and quickly turned my coat right-side out.

The rest of the week I made sure that not only my handouts, but also my clothing and my pockets, were ready for presentation.

~ Dorothy Floyd

❧ 22 ❧
I Got Confused

"Can you move the car back for me?" Daddy asked. He'd just finished cutting grass at the parsonage where we lived.

"Sure," I said. *How hard can it be? I may only be 10 years old, but living in the country, I'm able to sit in Daddy's lap and steer while he drives on some of the back roads. We've been doing this for years, so of course I know what I'm doing.*

I grabbed the keys and climbed in behind the driver's seat. I looked at the pedals and remembered one was for the gas and one for the brake.

"Pull up to the carport," Daddy said. I nodded my head in acknowledgement. The carport stopped where the back porch began. We had a red picnic table on the back porch where we gathered for picnics and evening meals when the weather is welcoming.

Taking a deep breath, I started the engine and put the car into gear. I began to coast forward and I felt good. "I can do this," I say.

I was fine until the time came to stop the car. "Now how do I stop?" I muttered. One was the brake and one the gas, but which was which? I pressed my foot down on the small pedal and the car sped up and headed for the porch.

"Stop!" Daddy yelled from the other side of the yard. I looked in the rearview mirror as he began to run across the yard.

"How do I stop?" I screamed out the open window, pressing the small pedal even harder. Maybe now I could stop! But I didn't. I just went faster and collided with the picnic table.

"Maybe I should try the other pedal," I thought. I moved my foot to the larger pedal to the left of my foot and pressed down. The car came to a stop, but it was too late. The damage was already done. I'd demolished our beautiful picnic table. There would be no more picnics or sandwiches outside. At least not in the near future.

"What did you do?" Daddy asked.

"I got confused," I admitted.

Sadly, we would repeat that question and response session numerous times in the coming years on a variety of topics and mistakes. This was one of many times when I misunderstood and my actions resulted in a stupid mistake. On other occasions, my rebellious nature intervened and I made other ludicrous and ill-advised decisions.

I'm thankful that our Father in heaven is a loving and forgiving God. He knows we're not perfect. After all, Romans 3:23 tells us all have sinned and fall short of the glory of God. Because of the redeeming blood of Jesus on the cross there is hope and restitution for our sins, great or small, in the atonement of Christ.

Jesus has revised and straightened out even the stupid mistakes I've made over the years. However, it's never been easy or the way I envisioned.

~ Diana Leagh Matthews

My daughter gave me a pair of deep-blue suede ankle boots for Christmas.

The left one always felt tighter than the right one when I put it on, but when I walked all was fine.

Then, one time my sock seemed to be wadded. I took the shoe off to smooth the sock, but it was already smooth. Curious, I felt inside the shoe and discovered the insole seemed to have come loose near the side of my little toe. I pushed it back down, and all was well, just still tight on my foot.

The next time I put the shoe on, however, it felt even stranger than usual. I reached inside and pulled out…cardboard…the cardboard lining that's put in new shoes to help retain their shape, and should be removed after purchase.

~ Yvonne

23

The Internet Date and the 23rd Psalm

For many people the 23rd Psalm is a favorite passage of scripture. It's a Psalm filled with hope and healing and one that is often quoted and memorized. I think I knew it by heart from the time I was a little girl.

While I know it and can quote it, the 23rd Psalm doesn't conjure up great memories for me. In fact, every time I hear any part of the 23rd Psalm I cringe and think back to a very bad, very embarrassing date.

Many years ago I found myself divorced with a young daughter. Internet dating was new at the time and many of my friends encouraged me to try it out. I signed up for a dating site and before long I met a man who lived near me, had a young son and even went to my church. Our church was very large, thousands of people, so it wasn't surprising that I didn't recognize him when I looked at his picture online.

We started talking by email and eventually he called me. We talked about our love for the Lord, our activities at church and reading the Bible. It was all going very well.

We decided to meet on a Sunday morning at church, sit together with our children and go out to lunch afterward. As Sunday drew near I started to get really nervous. I had never been good at dating and hadn't been on a date in a long, long time.

That morning I could barely brush my hair or put on makeup because my hands were shaking so bad. Driving to church I thought I might throw up. My daughter and I stood in the foyer at church looking expectantly around, while my stomach churned in agony.

Church started and no man with a young boy showed up. By that time I must have looked like I was having a nervous breakdown because even the church ushers and greeters were looking nervous and upset for me, and kept asking over and over if they could seat us.

It was official. I had been stood up on my date for church.

When we got home there wasn't a message on my phone but several hours later my no-show man called and apologized profusely, saying his son had gotten sick and that's why they didn't show up for church. While it felt a little weird, I accepted his apology and we agreed to meet the following week at church.

We talked a few times during that week and I could feel the nerves mounting again. My daughter had a friend spend the night on Saturday, and on Sunday morning we all got ready for *our* church date. The girls were excited about meeting the son and going out to lunch.

Once again we waited in the church foyer for what felt like an eternity. Church started and I thought I was being stood up again.

And then I saw them. My date looked like his online picture (a good sign) and his little boy was adorable. We made quick awkward introductions and hurried to find empty seats high up in the balcony.

As soon as I sat down I could feel my nerves kick into high gear. I was worried I wouldn't be able to talk if he asked me any questions. My date didn't seem nervous at all, and smiled at me a few times while we listened to the choir.

The choir started singing a version of the 23rd Psalm and it was obvious to everyone, including me, what Psalm was being sung. My date leaned over, smiled and said, "Do you know what Psalm this is?"

Then it happened. My mind went blank. Totally blank. I couldn't ask my daughter or her friend because that would have been too obvious. I searched the recesses of my brain and I finally came up with the fact that it was from the Psalms. Looking as stupid as I sounded, I muttered, "Yes, It's Psalm 25."

My date look dismayed and turned back toward the choir. I knew I had said the wrong Psalm but still couldn't remember. "Oh, I mean it's the 24th Psalm," I said, in a too loud and screechy voice. The people in the row in front of me glanced back at me with that "you need to be quite" look.

My date struggled to speak then turned to his son and whispered something. Then he leaned over and told me he was taking his son to the bathroom. I watched them slide out of the pew and that's when it dawned on me that it was the 23rd Psalm.

I tried to figure out what I would say when they got back from the bathroom. How would I explain that I was so nervous that my mind was blank but that I really did know the Bible and could even quote the 23rd Psalm.

I didn't have to worry about fixing my embarrassing moment. My date and his son never returned. Stood up again in church. Ditched in the balcony.

I explained to the girls what had happened as we walked out of church and headed to the car to go to lunch by ourselves. They laughed hysterically that I couldn't remember the 23rd Psalm, and all through lunch they quoted their own version to me: "The Lord is my shepherd, I shall not want…to meet an Internet date that stands me up…I shall not want to meet a date that ditches me in the church balcony…I shall not want to meet a man whose son has to go to the bathroom as soon as the choir starts singing."

I went to that church for several more years and never once saw the date who ditched me. While it turned out to be a very embarrassing experience for me, I also learned a valuable lesson.

The Lord is my shepherd, I shall not want…to date a man who can't find his way back from the bathroom.

~ Jan Westmark

❧ 24 ❧
Meow!

After two of my grandchildren shamed me into getting "a cute little kitten that would be homeless forever" if I didn't take him, I gave in and decided it was cute although I had more an affinity for dogs.

But I was trying, so I named her Sabrina, which means Princess, and called her Sabby.

By the time my fabric living room furniture had threads sticking out, the Christmas tree lost its trimmings, and my dog developed an inferiority complex, the kitten had grown on me simply because once a week, or maybe that was once a month, Sabby curled up near me as if she might let me live in the house with her.

To her credit, after tearing up my furniture she stopped clawing it. I learned "after" the fact how to train a cat, but I don't think I could have sprayed vinegar in her face or swatted her with a newspaper.

I'd never really expressed my almost-affection for Sabby, nor fully appreciated her until the afternoon we had a rare tornado warning. The sky grew dark as the television reporter warned us to find a safe place. The television went off. The lights went out. The air was oddly thick. Everything was eerily silent.

I prayed, "God help my spirit to be calm, keep me safe, and thank you for being with me." Then, while heading for the closet, I spied the cat reclining on the couch, looking at me and I said, "I'm so glad I'm not completely alone and have you, Sabby, somebody to talk to at times like this."

Uh oh! Then it hit me.

I had just talked to God, asking him to keep me safe. The next moment I acted as if that meant nothing and my safety resided in the claws of a cat.

I had to apologize to God for that one!

I didn't even bother to get into the closet then. I figured if I tried praying again, *someone* might tell me to just say, "Meow!"

~ *Yvonne Lehman*

❧ 25 ❧
The Prayer Stick

I was a middle-aged adult when I was saved by Jesus Christ while attending a local Baptist church.

Several years after my salvation, a friend and I went to a prayer rally for our city being held at a local Church of God. I didn't know much about their doctrine other than they believed in praying in tongues and could become quite boisterous during their worship. Neither of these bothered me as we are saved by the same Spirit and belong to the same Jesus, and I was excited to join them in intercession for our city.

During the prayer rally, the prayer leader would speak for a few minutes and then introduce a prayer point for the particular subject we were praying for. Different people throughout the sanctuary would pray out loud as the rest of us listened and prayed more silently in agreement. At one point during the prayers, my friend and I were kneeling at a pew and I felt the need to pray out loud.

As I was pouring out my heart before the Lord, my palms together in prayer, I felt someone slide a round-feeling object into my hands. Being in the throes of prayer, my mind focused solely on my Savior and what I was asking of him. The only thing I could imagine would be placed in my hand is what my mind considered a Prayer Stick. I figured it was for others to know who was praying. Therefore, I boldly raised my hand and the Prayer Stick high above my head so that all could see and continued my intercession for the people of my city. When I finished praying, I felt someone remove the Prayer Stick from my hand, and someone else took the lead in praying.

When the prayers on that particular subject winded down, we again stood to our feet. The prayer leader spoke for a few minutes and introduced another subject we were to pray about. As the praying began, I glanced around to see who had the Prayer Stick and what it looked like.

I didn't see anything, but I did notice the prayer leader as she walked toward the person who was praying out loud. Calmly, the prayer leader raised her arm and gently placed the...*microphone* into the woman's hand. I was mortified!

Instead of placing what I thought was a Prayer Stick into my hand, she had apparently placed a microphone into it; not so that others could know who was actually doing the praying, but so they could hear what was being prayed. There is no telling what went through the prayer leader's mind as I grandly held that microphone high above my head as I was praying.

I told my friend and she began laughing so hard she couldn't continue praying. The prayer leader didn't look at me again during that entire prayer rally. I was so embarrassed by what I thought she must be thinking. When it was over, I couldn't get out of there fast enough.

The following Wednesday at choir practice, I shared my embarrassing story with my choir and we all had a great laugh. The next Sunday, our children's minister walked up to me and handed me a brightly decorated toy karaoke microphone with streamers flowing down and the words Prayer Stick brightly painted on it.

It continues to be one of my most embarrassing, and funniest, moments.

~ Gloria Anderson

~ 26 ~
The Miracle Suit

Ever needed a miracle in your life — like right now? I found myself in this desperate situation when my son called to say his wedding, postponed the previous summer, was going to take place in one month.

One month!

I dropped my head into my hand and said, "Wonderful," all the while thinking, *There's no way I can lose enough weight to get in that dress in one month.*

In preparation for the first wedding, I'd lost 15 pounds and bought a beautiful, lavender dress. Even though my eyes had bulged at the price on the tag, I rationalized that my son's wedding was a once-in-a-lifetime occasion, so I'd splurged.

I'd had my beautiful dress altered, bought shoes and a handbag, and had them dyed to match. When I heard the news of the postponement, I pushed the dress to the back of my closet.

In the meantime feeling confident I could maintain my new weight, I stopped attending the weekly weigh-in meetings. Summer turned into fall and Thanksgiving feasts, fall into winter and Christmas parties, and winter into spring and Easter ham with the fixings. And I forgot all about weight watching — until I received the phone call from my son.

After saying goodbye and hanging up the phone, I made the long walk down the hall to my bedroom. I pulled the lavender dress from the closet, removed it from the hanger, took a deep breath, and pulled it over my head. Holding my stomach in, I *was* able to zip the dress, but as Forrest Gump said, "that's all I have to say about that."

In desperation I began working out and counting every calorie, determined to squeeze my body into that dress. Four weeks later, before packing the dress into a garment bag for the trip, I once again slipped it over my head. *Good enough,* I thought, *doesn't look like it did last summer, but it will just have to do.*

But, when the plane wheels touched down at DFW airport in Dallas where the wedding was to take place, the sudden altitude change evidently affected my brain. A vision flashed before my eyes of the groom's mother waddling down the aisle in a beautiful, lavender dress with bulges everywhere; around her waist, around her hips, and around her thighs.

Pushing fellow passengers out of the way, I frantically sought the Exit sign, while a single monotone word emerged from my mouth, "Mall. Mall. Mall…"

I dashed to the mall in search of the perfect slimming garment, and spotted a sign boldly proclaiming Miracle Suit. *Thank you, Lord, I needed a miracle and you sent it. You even called the thing a miracle suit.*

The label claimed the suit supports and enhances bust, flattens and slenderizes waist, and shapes and slenderizes hips and rear. I snatched that garment from the rack and practically danced my way into the fitting room.

God's Word tells us that Satan comes to steal, kill, and destroy. Well, this so-called miracle suit was supposed to *steal* those extra pounds from sight, but after about five minutes of trying to stuff my body into it, I feared it might be from Satan and kill and destroy me instead. I paused for a second, then the waddling vision flashed before my eyes again, and I resumed pulling and stuffing with all my might.

It suddenly became very hot in that fitting room.

I began sweating profusely, but I was determined to persevere. At that point, I reasoned, getting out of the thing wasn't going to be easy, so I might as well continue on.

In my excitement, I hadn't noticed if there was anyone else in the fitting area besides me. If there was, I realized, and they heard the moans and groans coming from my room, they might call 911 thinking someone was giving birth.

When the room began to turn black, and I saw little stars, I decided it was time for a break. I leaned my half-stuffed body up against the wall. *Whew. Why isn't someone coming around to check on those of us who are so innocently trying on these suits?*

I finally got the suit pulled all the way on, and to tell the truth, I couldn't see well enough, due to my now-bulging eyes, to know if my bust was enhanced, my waist slenderized, or my hips and rear shaped and slenderized. I also couldn't think clearly enough, due to the lack of oxygen going to my brain, to go put that suit back on the rack. So I bought it.

When I returned to the hotel room and pulled out my new purchase, everyone stopped what they were doing, and their mouths fell open.

"What is that?" my daughter asked. "It looks like a suit of armor."

I guess my mind suddenly adjusted to the altitude change, because I returned to a state of sanity. My daughter was right, the Miracle Suit did resemble a suit of armor. I did almost die trying to put it on. Instead of a gracious smile, I would most likely have a painful grimace on my face during the wedding. Forget smiling, I might not even be breathing. And by the time the reception rolled around, I could quite possibly be unconscious…but, I wanted my dress to look good!

I returned that miracle suit to the mall. The day of the wedding, I put on my dress and found that those huge bulges I'd imagined existed only in my panic mode.

Later I was able to laugh about the suit of armor I'd almost worn to my son's wedding. I've learned with a little discipline; physical, mental and spiritual, and with putting on the armor of God daily, I don't get myself into situations where I have to struggle with pleading to God for a miracle.

- Susan Dollyhigh

❧ 27 ❧
Expensive Chocolate Milk

I came home from work, was alone in the house, and fixed a snack. I sat in the living room, in front of the television, all ready for a relaxing time of eating and drinking. But suddenly, I knocked over my full glass of chocolate milk and it made a huge puddle and splashes on the carpet.

My wife wouldn't be home for a while and I wasn't sure what to do; I didn't know how to get it up. I watched it soaking into the carpet and knew it would get down to the pad.

Trying to ignore it, I decided to let it dry. After a while I could smell something like chocolate carpet. I'd heard that baking soda takes away odors. So I got the Arm & Hammer, sprinkled it liberally over the dried river of chocolate milk, got the vacuum cleaner and began to remedy my carelessness. Wife would never know.

But, the vacuum cleaner started making strange growling, threatening noises, then died. I took the bag out, looked inside and saw damp chocolate baking soda, mixed with some other debris. The clumps were imbedded in the brushes, the hoses...

I tried to clean it, but the contraption refused to do anything. It was no more adept at cleaning than I was.

For some strange reason the vacuum cleaner never worked again. I could have paid someone to come in and clean up for less than having destroyed a $250 vacuum cleaner.

The moral of the story — stupid vacuum cleaners can't do more than spit and sputter and leave discolored smears in the middle of the carpet.

We won't even talk about the price of a new carpet, or my wife's spitting and sputtering.

~ David A. Lehman

28
My Momma Taught Me...

My momma taught me from the time I was little, "The mouth can be your best friend, or meaner than the meanest man. Guard what leaves your lips."

She was right, too.

No one knew better than me, what it felt like to be an outcast. It wasn't enough to be skinny and somewhat homely, but add those blue cat-eye frames on top and my fate as a kid was sealed.

By college, I'd outgrown much of my outward awkwardness, but my mouth has always been clumsy. It was never something I set out to do — say stupid things or laugh a nervous laugh, but to this day, I'm very much haunted by it.

My most embarrassing moment happened after the birth of my first son. It was a hot Charleston, South Carolina dog day. My husband and I had attended Lamaze classes prior to my giving birth and in our weekly classes, we became acquainted with Melanie.

Melanie was a beautiful 23-year-old blonde who was muddling through a pregnancy with triplets. She wasn't expected to carry her babies to term but her doctor recommended she take the Lamaze classes to help prepare her for the birth process.

She was the sweetest woman. A continual spitfire filled with determination. But her five-foot-three-inch frame was as wide as it was tall as she carried her babies.

Four weeks into our Lamaze training, I went into labor and gave birth to a sweet baby boy. Since I was the first in our class to deliver, I never had the pleasure of going back to the classes to see all the young moms and their babies.

On an afternoon trip to a Charleston mall, I pushed my son in his stroller next to a circular rack of clothing. To my surprise, on the other side of the rack, was Melanie.

"Melanie, my gosh. How are you?"

"You started the labor wheel turning when you had your baby," she said.

We laughed, shared a few pleasantries and just before we were ready to part ways, Melanie stepped from behind the rack to hug me. That's when stupid hit.

Without a thought, I scanned her tiny body huge with triplets. "I see you're still hanging on. How much longer before the babies come?"

Melanie's face drew a blank as she pulled a stroller from behind the rack.

"There's no way I'm getting out of this one. No excuses. Nothing I can say to fix this." I felt my face grow warm.

Melanie burst into laughter. "I just had the babies last week. I'm afraid three babies and a small body will take some time to get back into shape."

"Last week! And you're out and about? I'm surprised you can still walk." As soon as the words left my mouth I knew I'd hit a double. It was bad enough to tell her she still looked pregnant, but to insinuate she shouldn't be able to walk after having three babies, only added insult to injury.

"Well, I've been insulted twice." Melanie broke into laughter. "It's okay Cin, I know what you mean."

"I should just hug you and leave, shouldn't I?"

"Naw. Just let me know how that foot tastes."

I can't remember a time I'd felt more stupid than I did that afternoon. My momma was right when she said our mouths can be our best friend or meaner than the meanest man. There was nothing I could say to make my blunder right. My mouth had already gotten me in trouble.

I often think of the words of Solomon when he uttered his wisdom: "**The words of the reckless pierce like swords, but the tongue of the wise brings healing**" (Proverbs 12:18 NIV).

Our words can be so reckless and once they are said, they can never be taken back — even when they are innocently spit out. I had no ill-intention toward Melanie. She was a darling. But I didn't take time to think through the words that would stab at her self-esteem. As innocent as the intention, it was a stupid and thoughtless mistake.

I'm grateful Melanie was such a joyful, Christ-filled woman. She quickly shared some much-needed grace and forgiveness, but I will always remember the moment the words left my mouth and the look of hurt on her face.

It's funny now, and I can joke that what made my face grow so hot in the mall was the dog days of a South Carolina summer. Over the years, I've remained in touch with Melanie. Her girls are grown and married now, and when she called to tell me her middle daughter was pregnant, she didn't fail to remind me of my after-pregnancy blunder.

Thirty-four years later, the words out of my mouth that day still embarrass me and rate as the world's stupidest moment.

I learned from that lesson and I continually remind myself of this prayer, "May the words of my mouth and the meditations of my heart be acceptable to You, Oh Lord, my Redeemer."

~ Cindy Sproles

29
Not Exactly the Smartest Things

A lot, if not all of us, have done some stupid things in our lives. Although the acts may not have been intentional they were not the smartest things to have done at the time. They may have occurred in a moment of stress when circumstances affected our logic. A kinder response should have been uttered but unfortunately it wasn't. Most of us have regretted such moments.

Later we realized what we said or did at that moment was not the smartest thing to say. It was dumb, ignorant, foolish, idiotic and imbecilic. It fact it was just plain *stupid*.

Sometimes we say things or do things that are illogical — like mopping up the floor while the faucet is still running. Another dumb thing would be touching a newly-painted wall, despite there being a sign saying — Wet Paint, Do Not Touch!

I remember hearing a parent shouting to her 11-year-old son who was cutting the grass for the first time. She yelled out the kitchen door, "Junior, be careful. Lawn movers can be dangerous." Ten minutes later she yelled again, louder. "Junior, slow down. Son, cutting grass can be dangerous." Half an hour later she lost her composure and screamed at him. "Junior, if you cut your feet off, don't you come running home to me!"

I was working part-time as a cashier at a supermarket during a forecast of a storm that would bring heavy doses of snow, ice, intermittent rain and heavy winds.

Having lived in the north, I found that northerners seldom blink an eye when a winter storm is approaching; but southerners seem to go into a panic mode. If southerners live in a mountainous region, their concern escalates even higher. They might get snowed in and be trapped on top of that mountain for days, or weeks. Therefore, it wasn't at all uncommon that in a matter of hours the supermarket would sell out of milk, bread, batteries, fire logs and other essentials.

During one storm alert, an elderly woman pushed her grocery cart to my register. Like many others, this cart was overflowing with groceries.

After ringing up four gallons of milk, I turned to her and teasingly said, "You won't have to worry about running out of milk, will you? You must love it."

She smiled and said, "No, not really. I never drink it, but I wanted to be ready just in case."

Well, I did ask.

In the movie *The Bucket List*, billionaire Edward Cole (Jack Nicholson) and car mechanic (Morgan Freeman) are complete strangers until fate lands them together in the same hospital. The men find they have something in common: a need to come to terms with who they are and what they have and have not done with their lives.

I have not yet come to the point where I feel it is necessary to write down some things I want to do before I pass away. On the other hand, I am certain the following list contains things that God does not want me to think, say, or do, as a follower of Jesus Christ.

My grandmother, a citizen of Spain, quoted Spanish Proverbs to me when I was a child. One was *"cosas estupidas que hago, pero no deberia hacer."* Translated it means "stupid things I do but should not do." It is just as applicable if reversed, describing those things I don't do, that I should do. That sounds like the sins of commission and omission. God's word agrees on both accounts!

Here are some foolish-versus-wise things I daily try to incorporate into my own life:

- It's foolish to not realize that walking the talk is more important than talking the talk. In other words…our actions speak louder than words.
- The way I drive (being courteous to fellow drivers and obeying the law) is a greater testimony than the Christian bumper stickers on my fender.
- The first thing on my daily To-Do List is my appointment with God.
- Not telling those closest to me that I love them (several times) daily is a failure.
- It is a nice gesture to complement those who have performed a task or

skill worthy of recognition but it is even better to compliment someone who performs a random act of kindness to a fellow human being. Years ago, Dr. Claude Frazier, a world renowned allergist, challenged me to daily do or say something nice to a person who went out of their way to serve another human being. That has become one of the most rewarding practices I've ever done.

- Don't ever walk away from any task until giving it my best effort.
- It is an indication of one's character to speak negatively about a person behind their back.
- Physical exercise is a good thing. According to 1 Timothy 4:8, it is even more important to exercise spiritually.
- A hasty decision may be a waste of time, money and energy. It also has the potential to destroy a relationship or someone's reputation.
- Your reputation is what others say about you but your character is who you really are.
- Judging another person and their actions before knowing the facts is faulty thinking. Try putting yourself in their situation and then evaluate the circumstances before judging.
- When you believe you do not have the time to help someone in need, you fail to realize that someday you might be that person in need.
- God expects us to joyfully assist children and the elderly who can't help themselves.
- A smile and a kind word to another may be the only act of love they will receive today.

- Tommy Scott Gilmore, III

∽ 30 ∾
All Thumbs

One day, with a friend in the passenger seat of the car, I pulled into a local gas station to top off my gas tank. It was one of the last remaining stations where they washed your windows while they filled your tank. My friend and I were chatting away and I had not been paying attention as the attendant filled the tank, wiped my windshield and fussed over us.

It was chilly, the car hadn't warmed yet, and I had on gloves. Without taking them off, when he came to the window and told me the cost, I fumbled around in my purse for the money I needed to pay him. Some dollar bills fell into my lap, and some change onto the floorboard, before I finally handed over several bills.

I joked to the man, "I'm sorry, I seem to be all thumbs."

"And I don't have any," he responded, holding up both his ungloved hands in front of my face. I stared at two hands with four fingers on each.

But…no thumbs!

I blubbered. "I didn't know. I am so sorry." Ramming my car in gear, I did not wait for my change. I was so embarrassed and felt so stupid for not noticing and hated to think that I had hurt his feelings. I didn't know whether to laugh or cry, so first I cried.

Eventually, once we had gotten far down the road, my friend and I laughed 'til we about peeded ourselves.

What were the chances?

- Diana Flegal

~ 31 ~
Front and Center

Chonda Pierce, Christian comedian, Queen of Clean was coming to a Lutheran church in Birch Run, Michigan. I hurried to get four coveted Golden Circle tickets for my husband, me, and two friends. The church secretary assured me that the Golden Circle tickets were front row seats…and I wanted to be front and center, just in case Chonda called on someone. I hoped it would be me. After all, I had written to her, saying that I was coming to see her and I was her biggest fan ever.

We decided to make a day of our trip to Frankenmuth, just outside of Birch Run. Our friend and her daughter would be driving themselves and coming later.

Frankemuth has the largest Christmas store in the world, and Zender's Restaurant and Gift Shop has the best chicken dinner ever. We ate like a king and queen, had a couple soft drinks, took a stroll to the River Place and bought an ice cream cone, meandered back to the car, and drove to the church.

We arrived in plenty of time and stood in line, which seemed like forever. Many ladies and some gents came in groups and started filling up the parking lot. The lines grew longer but I wasn't at all worried because I had Golden Circle tickets and as soon as those doors opened we were making sure we had our front row seats we were promised…until someone mentioned that Golden Circle tickets meant the first seven rows.

What? Not front row seats? But I had made sure we would have the seats closest to Chonda! Full-fledged panic set in. I was anxiety ridden. My husband tried to comfort me but this was my first concert and I was standing my ground, in Jesus name.

The doors opened and I rushed to the front row and wanted to grab the front row seats closest to the center aisle, almost dead center. I had told our friends that we would save them a seat but we could only get two seats close to the aisle because a man had taken the other two seats next to ours and refused to be kind enough to move a couple seats down.

So I uttered with an attitude, "Nice Christian manners" and he replied with the same attitude, "Sure is."

Frustrated, I asked a very nice lady if she would mind if we could take her seats and she humbly gave up her seats to accommodate us. I felt accomplished that I managed to get front and center seats, albeit in a sort of whiny selfish manner. Deep inside, I wanted Chonda to notice I was there, and that was that.

My husband sat in the first seat from the center aisle, I the second seat and our two friends next to us respectfully. Before the show started my friend's daughter and I went out to chat with Chera Kay, Chonda's daughter who was taking care of the sales table along with her boyfriend who had driven from Tennessee.

Back in our seats, we waited and then a man by the name of David Dean came out along with Chera Kay. He had driven from Indiana to stand in for Chonda because her plane had been delayed in Maryland and couldn't make it by seven and would be about an hour late. I was a little disappointed but as long as I was able to see Chonda I would be fine. They reassured us she was on her way, just be patient.

I had never heard of David Dean, but I can tell you this much, he is one of the funniest Christian comedians I have heard. He had us laughing so hard I forgot about my disappointment about Chonda not being there.

I had forgotten to go to the lady's room after eating and drinking so much soda before the show started. I had been laughing so much and so hard I just couldn't wait any longer; if I did, I would not only wet myself but probably those in my general vicinity. I whispered to my husband that I had…to go.

He said, well then go, that way, pointing to the left of us which meant I would have to sneak in front of about 20 people, one of them the rude fellow who I thought for sure would see me coming and put his foot out to trip me. So, with no time to spare I opted to silently sneak around my husband and make my way up the center isle towards my relief…until I heard, "Hey! Heeeey!"

I heard the "Hey" twice, but thought it just part of David's skit. I was so focused on getting to the ladies room without embarrassing myself that I ignored him.

Then I heard, "Heeeey, where do you think you're going?"

I quickly turned around to see that David had come down off the stage and was running toward me. *Oh my Lord*, I thought. He grabbed my hand and dragged me up on the stage and said, "Don't you know, that you never, ever, ever leave the room when a comedian is ready to give the punch line?"

I stood there with the deer-in-the-headlights look. I was speechless. The entire sanctuary was filled to the max and everyone was laughing very hard. It was like an out-of-body experience, if there ever was one. I was officially humiliated as I stood there, front and center.

Jumbotrons were ablaze with my red-flushed cheeks and trembling lips trying to utter anything that remotely sounded like a reply. He asked my husband, "Is she with you?" amid much laughter, then a pause.

"Yes," my husband replied.

Amid unbridled laughter, David looked at our friends. "She your friend?"

"Yes," they replied.

He paused, looked at me and said, "Ok, go get your friend and go pee."

I didn't just walk off that stage, I ran. As I opened the sanctuary doors to the open area, the youngsters who were selling water and other items were chuckling and snickering.

It's not funny. I'm humiliated beyond measure.

After my potty break, I didn't know what to do. Should I go back in or wait until David was done? Well, I couldn't just leave my husband and my friends. Surely the whole incident would be over so I might as well go back in.

So I straightened my shoulders, lifted my chin and marched back through the sanctuary door.

As soon as David caught sight of me coming down the aisle he yelled with great enthusiasm, "Pumpkin! You came back!" And he was rushing up the isle to welcome me. "Everything come out okay?"

I wanted to just melt away on the spot as he ushered me to my seat. Once I was seated, and David back on stage, I was able to regain my sense of humor. My husband and our friends just couldn't quit laughing. Secretly, I didn't blame them. It had to be hilarious from their perspective.

Mid-show break came and most people were out in the open area buying books and cds. That is when I spotted David behind a table selling some of his cds. I humbly went up to buy one.

He signed one and gave it to me. "You can come to my shows anytime you want to. You couldn't have had more perfect timing and you gave me great material to use!" he said.

"Great! I guess I am honored, um, I think…Thank you, Mr. Dean." I said.

Chonda finally showed up about an hour and fifteen minutes late. She was her usual funny self, and she said that she found it odd that as the limo was driving her from Detroit Metro Airport, she had been praying that the Lord would help them get there faster, which meant they were speeding.

"Doesn't quite seem quite right to pray for God to help you speed does it?" she said.

By then, I was quite content not to be noticed by Chonda. After the show, she held a meet and greet. I had bought her book and a couple of shirts I wanted her to sign, so I stood in line. This time, I politely waited my turn, acting a tad more Christlike, patience and all. I told her a little about my learning experience, she had a good laugh, signed my book and off I went. I adore that lady. She is such a real down-to-earth strong Christian gal.

God showed me the moral to this story not long afterward. He never fails to show us where we need to improve if we are open to His leading. I had wanted to be seen, acknowledged in the front row, front and center.

I was egotistical about it though. I found out later that the lady and her husband who gave up their seats to us were visiting pastors and part of David's show. I felt convicted. All in all, funny as it was, God, in a very clever way, gave me my heart's desire, just not quite the way I wanted it.

We look back on it now and we still laugh about the incident. I thank God that He has a sense of humor. I can picture Him sitting on the edge of heaven saying, "You want to be the center of attention do you? Ok, as you wish."

It just proves that when we force our way we will get what we probably deserve but if we stay humble and let God bring us up front and center, it will be the right way. God will raise us higher.

~ Maggie Micoff

✌ 32 ✌
Surrender to Laughter

I waved to the driver as the school bus pulled away. Seconds later the children came bounding across the yard, crunching colorful fall leaves. Will, with all the energy of a first grader, hopped onto the front porch, said a quick "Hi, Mom," and disappeared into the house, leaving his backpack at the front door. Julianne, four years older, trailed a bit slower.

Eying my son's backpack reminded me to check for notes or homework. While shuffling through the papers, I found a picture Will colored of himself crying. The words below the picture said, "I hate it, I hate it, I hate it when my sister tells me what to do." My heart was wounded. Because of the seriousness of the matter, I knew it was time to intervene. I invited Julianne to sit down with Dad and me at the kitchen table.

Julianne's long red hair framed her freckled face. She had a sweet, innocent look about her, but also a curious one.

"I found this in your brother's backpack," I began. Glancing at the picture, tears formed in Julianne's eyes.

"I only tell him what to do to keep him from doing something stupid," she whispered.

About this time I heard a noise at the door and I suspected that Will had been listening. I gently opened the door and predictably, Will fell through. I asked him to join us at the table to continue the conversation.

"Will, how does this make you feel?" I asked with pride, as I just knew this was the perfect "James Dobson" moment, openly discussing and resolving the conflict.

Will looked intently into my face, his blue eyes wide. "I just hate it when she tells me what to do." I explained a few things while Will continued to focus on my face. I felt certain he was gaining new insight into the dynamics of family. *This is going so well,* I thought.

"Do you understand what I'm saying?" I asked.

Very inquisitively Will's mouth fell open and his brow wrinkled as he stared at me. I just knew something profound was about to flow from his sweet little lips. And then it did.

"Mooooooooooom," he said slowly. "Do you *know* you have a mustache?"

I gasped and quickly covered my mouth with my hand. It was then I knew he hadn't heard anything I had said. My victorious teaching moment was shattered! Dad laughed so hard that he fell off the kitchen chair and onto the floor. Julianne's laughter brought fresh tears. Will glanced around from one to another, his facial expression asking, *What did I say?*

The roaring laughter was contagious and I surrendered to it. Dropping my hand from my face I laughed 'til I cried. Even Will began to giggle.

After the laughter died down, we relaxed. The previous mood had changed. The unanticipated eruption of our laughter made our problem appear less detrimental. The kids' laughter opened the door for bonding and trust and rekindled all our playfulness. And for Julianne, her guilt became a glimmer of hope when she knew her parents were supporting her.

The benefits of laughter are widely publicized. Paul E. McGhee, PhD, an expert in laughter therapy, writes "Humor lightens your burdens, inspires hopes, connects you to others, and keeps you grounded, focused and alert."

God, the Creator of our bodies and minds, also says something about laughter. Proverbs 17:22 tells us a joyful heart is good medicine. (NASB)

So go ahead. Laugh. Laugh often. Set the example for laughter in your home. It will free your children to find humor in their own situations, especially the problems. Most of all, laughter bonds families, whether you have a mustache or not!

~ Debbie Presnell

33
Let Them Eat Cake

Fresh out of college and working my first job, I sometimes went out with my co-workers at the end of the day just to get to know people. One evening we went to a restaurant and, because the place was busy, we had to wait in the bar for a table. While everyone else began unending beers and mixed drinks, I ordered a soda. I wasn't trying to be "holier than thou;" I had simply never cared for the taste of alcohol.

While we mingled there in the bar, I was approached by someone I recognized but had never met. He wasn't a co-worker but had recently moved into an apartment a few doors down from mine. He introduced himself and we talked for a moment. "Hey," he said, "I'm having a cake party at my place on Saturday. Want to come?"

A cake party? My imagination was fired up at once with an image of what a cake party must look like. Surely, a confectionary lover's delight! Angel food cake with strawberries, delectable devil's food cake with delicious chocolate icing, bunt cake, pound cake, upside down cake, ice cream cake, cupcakes with colorful sprinkles on top. Perhaps there would even be piles of perfect little petit fours presented on silver platters.

Say no more, I thought. I didn't need to be asked twice. I told my new neighbor I'd be there.

Saturday came and at the designated hour I ventured on over to Apartment 1320. The door was open, music played and a crowd had begun to gather inside. Being naturally shy, I lingered in the doorway a moment and looked around. It was then I noticed that something was terribly wrong.

There was not a single cake inside this man's apartment. No sheet cakes, no cupcakes, no double layer cakes with mounds of icing. Not even one lonely petit four growing stale on a paper plate. Just huge dispensers of beer at several strategic points around the room. And stacks of plastic red Solo cups to dispense it into.

As my taste buds crumbled in despair, understanding dawned.

This wasn't a cake party at all. It was a keg party!

Quickly, before anyone so much as knew that I was there, I was gone, slinking away with my tail between my legs, like a puppy without a bone.

~ Ann Tatlock

❧ 34 ❧
Stupid or Pretty Smart?

When I heard about writing a story about stupid moments, I had difficulty trying to determine which of my many, many stupid occurrences would be appropriate. One that could have ended my life might grab your attention and leave you shaking your head at my naïveté, or wondering if this stupid moment was really quite smart!

Some years ago I joined my husband on a business trip to Colorado. He was meeting with a client just outside of the city of Denver and I had the entire day by myself to explore an area I had never before visited. My husband, being the considerate man that he was, rented a white full size Lincoln. Long ago, *full size* meant really, really big.

I dropped Dave off at the company he was calling on at 8 a.m., assuring him I would be back at 5 p.m. to pick him up.

Besides being the days of really big cars, those were also days before iPhones, expansive cell service, or GPS. So, with a map I had taken from a rack in the lobby of our hotel, no cell phone in my purse, and in a strange car, I was off on my great adventure.

I started off to find The Teller House, in Central City, the location of the *Face on the Barroom Floor*, painted in 1936 by Heron Davis. A poem of the same name, written in 1872 by Hugh Antoine D'Arcy had had always haunted me. It is a story about a man who fell in love and whose life eventually was ruined, to the point of death, by the object of his great affection. The face at Teller House is of the artist's wife, "Nita" Davis, and not the object of the poem.

Driving to Central City I took a wrong turn and ended up on an Indian Reservation where I drove through miles of nothing but loose, powdery snow in a barren and desolate landscape. Eventually I was able to turn around and correct my path. Arriving at The Teller House, and realizing I was not the last human who remained on earth, I found the painting, which was not as exciting as I had built it up in my mind to be. I resisted the temptation to drop coins in a slot machine and, after grabbing a quick sandwich and a cup of hot tea, headed out to find the Vail ski resort, about an hour from my location.

The Rocky Mountains were indescribable. Big, bold, tall, rocky, black — those were the words that came to mind as I watched them through my windshield. When I saw a sign announcing "Mountain Pass," the words seemed to be begging me to be adventuresome. Turning onto the two-lane road, my white Lincoln began the climb. Soon I was a little troubled by the numerous 'S' turns, steep incline, narrow road, no guardrails, and falling snow. Similar to my time on the Reservation, I hadn't seen a car in front or behind me since entering the Pass. I had no idea how deep the snow was until my car refused to climb further. With a slight 'fish tail' of the back tires, the car refused to climb further. Putting the car in park I opened the door, discovering the snow was above the bottom of the door panel. What was I thinking? How stupid was this idea to ride a Mountain Pass in the Rockies, in the middle of winter, in a place where no one knew I was.

I was scared. If this white car went over the side, slipping into the crevice of the dark valley of nothingness below, I would not be found until the spring thaw. I began to shake. Then I began to pray. Earnestly, I begged God to get me back to level ground, unharmed, in one piece. I got back in the car, looked up toward heaven, and with great resolve put the car in reverse and began creeping backwards. I have never felt so stupid in my entire life. I have also never before felt my life was in such imminent danger. I was totally dependent on the Lord to get me out of this one.

He did. I continued to back slowly down the road, until an area a little wider than the two lanes came into sight. I did what I'd learned to do before I took my driver's test — little did I know at that time how important knowing how to do a three-point turn would be. Finally, heading down the mountain looking out the windshield rather than the rear window I began to breathe a little easier. The snow lessened and the road became somewhat clearer the lower I descended. Finally the beautiful little village I had passed through before entering the Pass came into sight. I was never so happy to see anything in my life.

When I picked up David, about an hour later, he got in the car with these words, "Did you hear about the 90-car pile-up on the interstate between here and Vail?" My head swiveled as I looked at him with shock on my face. "Really? I almost went there this afternoon and probably would have been caught right in the middle of that, if I hadn't decided to climb a Mountain Pass instead."

He looked at me and grinned. "Well, Hon, I always did say that you were one smart woman. Although I've also had the guys at the plant tell me to never get on a Mountain Pass this time of year."

I almost laughed. It wasn't until hours later that I told him how truly "unsmart" my going up the Pass had been, or had it?

~ Toni Armstrong Sample

❧ 35 ❦
Do You Read and Write?

The tongue can get us into a lot of trouble. Words come out unedited. When my publisher for my *Titanic* book came to spend the day at my book signing at the *Titanic* Display in Pigeon Forge, Tennessee, she and her husband took me and my friend out to dinner.

When the conversation turned to books being read and written I looked at the publisher's husband and asked, "Do you read or write?"

"I do both," he said.

Oh, I felt so ridiculous, having wanted to make a good impression as an intelligent, successful author. I failed.

Fortunately, everyone laughed good naturedly, knowing I was referring to the writing process, which requires a lot of both reading and writing.

But that reminds me of the many times (every time) that I'm trying to write my story in a way the reader will enjoy, I feel like a failure.

A while back I emailed my agent with the words, "Everyone is going to find out I'm not really a writer."

He emailed back, "Ha. Ha. When that email came in, I was on the phone with another client who was saying the exact thing, that she's not a writer and never will be."

I'm now written my 56th novel. But only once in this writing business, did I ever feel like a "real" writer during the process, and that was with my 50th novel, *Hearts that Survive – A Novel of the Titanic*. From the time the editor said, "Yes, if you can do it in a short period of time," I wrote the first draft, 120,000 words in six weeks and it required very little editing. My craft and creativity came together in a remarkable way. I felt it flowed.

All the others have required work, and time, and change, and editing and wondering if I'm a real writer. After each book is finished, I'm surprised that the effort came together and I can remind myself that I am a writer, one who works hard in this profession.

When I begin reading a book, I think of all the time and effort that went into getting those words down and realize again how much effort this and any profession requires. And I'm so grateful for readers.

I can read. I can write. And am so glad I don't have to "speak" my novels.

- Yvonne Lehman

※

This really happened at my church.
The visiting quartet was singing, "Jesus is all I need,"
while the ushers were passing the plate
throughout the congregation
for the quartet's love offering.
- Yvonne

~ 36 ~
I Could Have Been a Contender if I Hadn't Had a Jesus Crush

Yep. Did it. Wrote about the time I wore a red jumpsuit and sashayed into a pop star's concert. Front row seats. Toted binoculars. I was there to ogle this sexy gyrating star busting a move. I thought he was the greatest dancer who'd ever lived. He could shake a leg better than Elvis.

Years later when I began writing, I wrote about the event for a writing contest. All in jest. I didn't have to embellish too much while keeping the story within the confines of creative nonfiction. It is true, however, that the star bumped and grinded all the way over to my side of the stage and that my girlfriend leaned over and said, "He's singing to you" and I replied, "Yes, I know," without taking my eyes off the idol.

I entered that story in a humor contest, wondering if my humor was funny enough to place. What, exactly, did it take to write humor, which was considered difficult by many? After the contest, I intended to give the story a quick burial. I was not particularly proud of this story. Well, maybe I was because it *was* pretty funny. This contest was for a secular conference and before God had totally convinced me I needed to be writing for him.

The humor judge was the same lady critiquing our manuscripts. She told me, "You have to take out, 'That was before my to-think-it-in-your-heart-is-the-same-as-committing-the-sin days.' Sounds like a Jimmy Carter statement."

"I can't take that sentence out. My entire story hinges on that one line!"

"Well," she said, "people won't laugh. And, you need to take out Priapus-worshippers. Your readers are rednecks. They won't get it. Even *I* don't know what that means."

Like, c'mon. Rednecks don't own dictionaries or know how to Google? Let 'em do some research and find out why God was so angry in the Old Testament.

After she'd cut it down to newspaper column size, she shoved it at me. "Read this open mic night."

Horrified, I said, "I can't read that out loud — In Public!"

"Oh, c'mon."

Well, from her pressuring me to read it, maybe she liked it a little. Maybe it had an honorable mention chance.

But what about my reputation? I'd be labeled "Scarlet Woman."

I lost sleep.

Tossed and turned for most of the night.

Prayed.

After God let me suffer through a thousand imaginary upside down crucifixions with added fire, in the stillness of the early morning I heard in my heart, *Go ahead. Read it. I'll turn it around for good. Later, you can witness about how you love Jesus.*

My voice quivered as I said, "God, that had better be you."

With fear and trembling I wore red. Swiped on matching lipstick for a visual.

Ratcheting up courage, I stepped to the microphone, feeling like Miss Melanie Hamilton on the inside, looking like Miss Scarlett O'Hara on the outside. I stood before God and a redneck audience — according to the contest judge — reminiscing about lusting after a pop star in skin-tight pants.

Surprised myself.

Belted out lyrics. "Whoah, whoah, whoah."

Said, "I looked hot."

"I was hot."

(Like one writer friend once said, "Well, we were all hot back then!")

But my daughter later said, "Mom, I can't believe you wrote that!" She was mortified.

I replied, "Darlin', I was young once and wore a size four before you and your sister came along and wrecked my miry temple of clay."

Okay, I'm regressing to keep from telling the worst part. But here's the rest of the story. After I saw the "star" kissing all of those women carrying Champagne bottles and long-stemmed roses up to the stage for a lip-lock, I thought, gross! No way was I going to be lured to the spotlight and swap spit with all of those lusting women. Where, in that idol's lifetime, had those sweet lips been? A bulldozer couldn't have pried me off my seat for a kiss even if they'd paid me.

Then here's what happened later at open-mic-night.

While I was reading my story, laughter tinkled in all the right places.

If the rednecks didn't know what Priapus meant, they laughed anyway, went home and looked up the word, and learned why God hates idols. And when I talked about "that was before my to-think-it-in-your-heart-is-the-same-as-committing-the-sin days," my audience laughed there too, and I figured they all must have voted for Jimmy Carter and bought his books, or perhaps they were laughing at him and not with him, which wasn't very nice either.

But I lived through that travesty without God calling down lightning to strike me dead or sending in a hoard of toads. So I figured that was truly God I heard from the night before, though I was kinda peeved at him for letting me wrestle with my dilemma and lose sleep 'til two in the morning.

The next day, during lunch break at the conference, I strolled to the lunchroom, went through the line for red snapper, and set my tray down on a table. A guy was already there and I saw his name on his nametag. Being friendly, I introduced myself. With no hint of laughter in his voice, but with humorous undertone and twinkling eyes, he replied, "Oh, I know who you are." Long pause. "And I will *never* forget you."

He wore a long ponytail. Looked like the literary type. It could have been he was there incognito as a redneck. I refrained from pulling back his collar to check because I didn't want him checking mine. Who was I kidding? He already knew the color of my neck after open-mic night. He'd obviously been there to witness my confession of the night before.

I glanced at a couple of Rome acquaintances sitting at the next table over — not the Rome across the big pond but the Rome south of the little pond below Tennessee and east of Alabama. I let out an embarrassed laugh. A nervous laugh. A where-do-you-want-a-door-in-that-wall-because-I'm-getting-ready-to-make-one laugh.

Everybody else laughed *hearty* laughs. Glad-it-was-you-instead-of-me laughs. My face flamed blue it was so hot and I asked those within shouting distance, "Have you not ever done anything stupid in your younger days?" Harmonizing, the Georgia Peach girls quipped, "Well yeah, but we don't talk about it."

Desperate for approval and trying to save myself, I said, "Do you still love me now you know I lusted?"

The peaches sang out acapella, "Only 'cause Jesus tells us to!"

A big toothy grinned guy said, "That was a great story you read last night! You had me blushing and chuckling. I'd heard about women being aggressive these days, but I didn't know how far you were gonna take that." He invited me to move into his new resort community on the coastal waters of the Atlantic. Invited me to go with him to cast line. He could have been a fishing pervert. One never knew. (Turned out he was happily married and only trying to sell real estate lots in a coastal neighborhood — whew!)

I said, "Remember hoss, it's *creative* nonfiction. The entire story hinged on that one line: that was before-I-knew-to-think-it-in-my-heart-was-the-same-as-sinning days."

I kept thinking, *God, I can't believe you encouraged me to act like a fool — oh yeah, you put Jeremiah through the wringer too. Anyway Lord, I will never live this down.*

At the end of the conference on awards night, as the honorable mention was called, I was disappointed because my story hadn't won. It didn't even take third. Then didn't take second. I'd acted like an idiot for — practice.

Then, I heard my name.

Whoah, whoah, whoah!

And yes, the scarlet woman wore red down the carpet to accept her first place award for "I Could Have Been a Contender."

But that wasn't the end of the story. I later wrote another story about writing the first story which became "My Redneck Summer" which won first place in an international contest. And I've used these stories to speak to many people about Christ and how most of us have done stupid things in our youth before we matured and dove deeper into God's word.

And God did indeed do as he'd promised that night of my tossing and turning. He turned my foolishness around for good. Romans 8:28 tells us, "We know that God causes all things to work together for good to those who love God, to those who are called according to His purpose."

I still have the red jumpsuit, but only to remind people of my stupidity.

My daughter loaned it to one of her few girlfriends who could squeeze into a size four and she wore it to an 80's party with a blouse underneath. All of her friends heard about my pop idol story and the writing contest and my winning performance. Isn't it amazing how God can really turn a sow's ear into a silk purse and everything works out to glorify him.

I now pray without ceasing Psalm 25:7, "Remember not the sins of my youth, nor my transgressions: according to thy mercy remember thou me for thy goodness' sake, O Lord."

~ *Vicki H. Moss*

37
Who Died?

Several years ago I had an opportunity
To reach out to a grieving family through my gift of poetry
I saw in the paper a lady had passed away
I thought it was my friend's mother so I began to pray
I said Lord tell me what I can do and he spoke to me and said
Go minister to the family of the one that's dead
I went to the funeral home but when I walked inside
I'd never seen those people or the lady who had died
I went and signed the guest book and an usher came to me
I said I didn't see the person I went there to see
He told me she would be there when the morning came
So he pointed out her brother although I didn't know his name
We talked for a few minutes about the peace on his mother's face
After suffering so long she finally won the race
He asked me if I could come back for the funeral the next day
I told him I would be there and for him I would pray
When they brought the casket in with the family behind
I still didn't see my friend but it didn't cross my mind
I sat through the service then followed to her resting place
I walked up to her brother and the color left my face
He thanked me for coming and I said his sister I'd not seen
When he pointed to this woman she was tall, blonde and lean
Then suddenly it hit me the family I didn't know
So I got in my car and drove as fast as I could go
On the way back to the house I said Lord what have I done
That's when I heard him laughing and knew he was having fun
He did stop laughing long enough at the end of the day
And said you did what I asked you to and I led you all the way
The moral of this story is make sure you know who died
Then you won't have the urge to run and find a place to hide!

~ Joye Atkinson (aka The Funeral Crasher)

~ 38 ~
iSwim at the Beach

I love family vacations. Those great memory making caravan trips when the entire family agrees to meet at a planned destination for a few days and by some amazing miracle — or 20 — we look back and smile after everyone enjoyed (almost) every minute of the trip no one originally wanted to take — except for me, the trip cheerleader, of course.

This phenomenon is rare enough, but soon after I booked the reservations for three beachfront balcony suites at a four star resort on Lido Key, and told my husband, "We only have two toddlers, one five-year-old, three married couples, a teenager, and a bachelor staying in three huge suites. I'm sure it will be great." He agreed to go with only a minor argument. Now *that's* rare in the *rarest* sense.

My husband, Dennis, raised his eyebrow and made a sickly coughing sound when I gave him the printed confirmation with the grand total. "You're kidding me, right?"

I said, "No," and assured him we wouldn't spend much money for food, souvenirs, or anything else.

He gave me the; I-know-you're-fibbing look, and said, "Would you like some cheese with that whine?"

I didn't laugh. I promised mid-August is a great time to take a vacation.

"You usually say mid-October is a great time to take a vacation. Are you sure you don't want to go to the mountains this fall?"

He knows I always want to go to the mountains, so I pretended not to hear him. "Everyone can get to the beach in a few hours." I reluctantly agreed there would be no frivolous gift shop stops or fancy dinners on this trip. "It's summer. Most of the family is dieting." I pointed to a group of hard bodies on the brochure. "See? People don't eat at the beach. It's a well known fact."

I managed to convince him. But then, I said the cursed words I'd regret long after that memorable trip. "Trust me, Dennis, we won't spend a penny over the resort rates on this trip, and I'll stick to a strict budget until Christmas."

"Can I have that in writing?" He said and laughed. "We'll go, but you tell the kids the trip is our gift for all their upcoming birthdays. Deal?"

"Deal!" *Wait? Is he kidding?*

Knowing I had to hold to the promise *we wouldn't spend frivolously*, I packed everything except the kitchen sink; Sunscreen to cover 10 horses (I mean, people), food, low-cal snacks for six weight watchers, board games, swimsuits for two pale guys who probably wouldn't swim, and a few necessities for me — four hats, three pairs of sunglasses, and six headbands for three days.

I also needed a container for all the shells I hoped to find, so I took an extra suitcase and two large black trash bags.

When we arrived at our destination, a balmy sea breeze welcomed us. The icing on the cake for a last minute vacation to one of Florida's beautiful west coast beaches.

I stood ready, snapping photos with my phone at every turn. I took great shots of my daughters-in-love, Faith and Valery, running along the shore with their children, the kids splashing and giggling, riding the waves, and the sandcastle we built at sunset. I shared tons of photos on Facebook: pictures of birds, shells, people. A few people who looked like birds, and everything in between. I think I might have taken pictures of my foot, the car floor mats, and the yellow lines in the parking lot too.

A midnight storm and the current moon cycle meant great shelling during the next low tide. I planned to meet Valery on the beach at sunrise the next morning. I grabbed my phone, mesh bag, and off I went into the darkness. Once at the shore, I kicked off my flip-flops, stuck everything in the open weave bag, and headed in to the knee-deep water.

Within minutes I had collected some of the most magnificent shells I'd ever seen in 30 years of combing Florida's shores. "Oh my goodness! This is great!" We both waded deeper, and then along the edges of a rocky jetty which held sand dollars, fish, and a few small fragments of aged sea glass. We'd hit the mother lode, or died and gone to seashell heaven. I swung my arms — and then my bag — through the warm waves. I celebrated with my version of the happy dance until Valery looked at me wide eyed like she saw a ghost, or worse, a shark.

"What's wrong?"

Looking at my submerged bag, she asked, "Where's your phone?"

We were still in thigh-high water. My scream mingled with the sound of water crashing against the jetty. "Oh noooooo!"

A nearby fisherman looked toward us and waved. *Did he think I said hello?*

I lifted my dripping bag out of the surf and tried to smile when Valery waved thumbs up back to him. "I bet he thought we saw a shark."

My heart sank when I looked at the soaked bag. "I'd be better off if I did."

Shells, bent flip-flops, and my shimmery gold iPhone peeked though the tiny holes in the bag. "How am I going to tell Dad I took my phone in the ocean with me?"

"Turn it off and put it in a bag of rice as soon as possible," Valery said, "It'll be okay after a few days."

Her positive attitude consoled me while we walked back to the hotel. In those few minutes of silence, my heart cried out to God.

Oh, Lord, how can I explain this costly stupid mistake to Dennis? There's no way he's going to understand, especially since this isn't the only dumb thing I've done with phones and water. A year hasn't passed since my other new phone went swimming, albeit in our home — in a much smaller ocean of sorts. — And You know, Lord, I had a hard time explaining that incident without laughing.

As we neared the lobby entrance an awful feeling came over me. I imagined the look of disappointment on my husband's face. Doubt tugged at my thoughts. I dreaded hearing him say, "I told you so," and I imagined a Mr. Know it All smirk on his face. A sea of positive explanations collided with waves of negative answers in my brain... *See, this is why some wives don't tell their husbands about two stupid mistakes in a row. Your husband might want you to read something called Smart Phones for Dummies...*

A frigid slap of air blindsided me when Valery opened the heavy glass door. She stepped aside to let me in. "It's okay, Mom," she said, "Dad will understand."

Once on the elevator, I closed my eyes. It sped to the eighth floor. The sudden tingle of goose bumps covered me — but not like a blanket. I imagined God sitting on a fluffy cloud. Though I couldn't see his face, somehow I thought he smiled and winked at me. This split second vision of God-wink dust sprinkling down on me from heaven warmed my heart. Again, I poured out my concerns to him. *I'm a middle-aged woman and I still do childish things…*

A familiar quiet voice soothed my soul and calmed my mind; *I see the depth of all your mistakes, silly or serious. Dennis loves you almost as much as I do. Trust he will too.*

And Dennis did.

He hugged me, wiped my tears away, and laughed at the visual of me swinging my bag of shells through the waves. He knew taking the phone to the beach was a careless choice on my part. And a new phone would put us way over budget after this impromptu family vacation I instigated. But, my husband, like my heavenly father, chose to look at the depth of my silly mistake. He looked at the smiles of our family in the many photos I luckily shared before my phone went swimming with the fishes that morning. He chose to see the story behind the stupid moment we'll laugh about for years to come.

I'm beginning to think these moments add color and vibrancy to the memory of our lives. After all, time plus a little God wink dust always equals something extraordinary. Someday, when we look back at a few of these stupid moments in our lives, hopefully, we'll see beautiful memory moments.

I also received my birthday present early this year. A new shimmery gold iPhone and ugly life proof case. Just in time for fall, and perhaps another family trip…to the mountains.

~ Joann M. Claypoole

39
Sir, Have You Been Drinking?

While driving to work one morning, I unknowingly passed a cop. As hard as it is to believe, I wasn't really going all that fast and was pretty much staying with the traffic flow. After all, how fast can you go in morning rush hour traffic?

Well, it happened to be an unmarked police car and I didn't see it or recognize it. As I passed by, I heard a car start honking at me.

Guess how well I respond to that?

I mean…early morning traffic combined with a foggy, pre-caffeinated brain, the usual impatience and my mind on the workday ahead!

The car sped up and I looked over two lanes of traffic to visually confront my early morning nuisance. I saw a burly, bald-headed guy in the car waving his arms and angrily pointing at me.

Guess how well I respond to that?

I scowled at him, made some kind of shoulder shrug and continued to move along with traffic. Yes, you guessed right — blue lights and siren blaring right behind me.

We stopped at the next red traffic light as there was no side street, shopping center or even a convenience store on that miserable stretch of road. From my rearview mirror I saw him get out of his car and head my way. As he approached my now open window, I asked him if he wanted me to pull over at the next intersection. After all, we were in the middle of three lanes of morning rush hour traffic and I was (insert sarcasm here) deeply concerned for the safety of the other drivers. To be honest, I was embarrassed and wanted to take our early morning circus to a quiet side street. He said, "Nope — we'll handle this right here!"

He asked for my license and registration. So I rummaged through the glove compartment looking for the current year's registration and then slid what I thought was my license out of my wallet. Upon looking over what I had given him, he asked me "Sir, have you been drinking?"

At around 6:45 in the morning? Remaining calm and in control, I laughed and said, "No, why?" not understanding why he would ask such an unusual question at that time of day.

He said, "Well, I asked for your license and you handed me your debit card."

My first thought was, *Does he honestly think I'm trying to bribe him to get out of whatever ticket he was going to give me? If so, he'd better have one of those card-swipey things for his smart phone!*

I told him my debit card is the only thing I ever pull out of my wallet — must have been a habit. What followed was one of the most bizarre, rapid-fire conversations I've ever had.

He asked if I didn't notice the police car. I said, "Nope, it looks like any other car to me."

He asked if I didn't see the big antennas on the car. I said, "Nope I wasn't paying attention" (meaning, not paying attention to his car). Exasperated, he interrupted me and asked if I normally don't pay attention when I'm driving. I laughed and said, "Yes, I pay attention — just wasn't paying attention to your particular car."

He then asked if I couldn't see him pointing to the speed limit sign. I said "No, I thought you were just another angry morning commuter who was mad for being in the slow lane."

He asked if I couldn't see his patch on his uniform that says "police" on it. Now at this point in the conversation, my mind immediately wanted to express something like, "I can't even see faces at that distance" or "No, you could be a Rent-a-Cop Security Guard for all I know." But something inside advised against demonstrating my snappy brilliance at that point and time of my life.

Once I realized what I had done, we made the exchange — my license for my debit card — and he went to his car to pull up whatever information he could find on me. After about three minutes of cars whizzing by us in the other two lanes and cars backing up behind us in our lane, he returned to say, "Mr. Stevens, up here in North Carolina we pay attention. Do you think you can pay better attention when you're driving?" I happily and quickly agreed.

He asked me where I worked, so I gave him my employer's name in downtown Charlotte. He asked me what building I worked in and I told him. He finally handed me back my license and registration and asked me to be more careful in the future.

Then I did something I've never done before or thought I would ever do. I stuck my hand through the window and shook his hand, smiled, and thanked him! As I drove off, ignoring the staring, angry, impatient drivers all around me, I burst out in laughter as I replayed the entire situation in my mind! No, I hadn't been drinking; but I hadn't been paying attention either.

I am thankful God has a sense of humor. I am also deeply grateful He is patient enough to continue working on me, molding me more and more into His likeness each day and in every situation.

Even when I'm not paying attention.

~ Nate Stevens

∞ 40 ∞
A New Windshield

I know my transgressions, and my sin is ever before me.
Psalm 51:3

One frigid January morning, Tom scraped my windshield. I had an early-morning appointment, and I was running late. By the time I crawled into the car, the windshield had iced over again. The scraper wasn't in its spot, so I frantically grabbed a small metal box from my purse. It worked great and I was on my way.

Two days later, I was petrified as I drove facing the sun. There was a scratch on the glass. Not just one scratch, but multiples. My husband is quite fussy about his vehicles, and I dreaded telling him.

The men in the therapy clinic had plenty of advice.

"Call SafeLite. They will come to you now and fix it and your husband will never know."

"Why didn't you use a credit card?"

One even went outside to *see*. "Yes, I would kill my wife," he said with a grin.

I couldn't concentrate on the therapy session because I knew I was doomed. Thankfully, my husband didn't *kill* me. Neither did he berate or blame me. Even as I cried and begged forgiveness, he hugged me. "It can be fixed." We had hoped it could be buffed with a coating, but the scratches were many and some too deep. This would cost more money.

I continued to criticize and condemn myself. How could I have been so irresponsible? What was I thinking, or why wasn't I thinking? Every single time I sit in that car, I am faced with the consequence of my careless, thoughtless actions. Those scratches seem to go deeper and deeper.

Soon my car will have a new windshield, and I will be freed of my guilt over this costly act. I will remember every time I look through that glass how costly my mistake was. I have a new understanding of my sin "ever before me." No matter how many times I try to rub away the scratches, I can't. Apart from replacing the windshield, I have no hope.

God, in his amazing grace and mercy, has forgiven me my sins. As I come to Him in tears of sorrow, He reaches down and removes all my scratches. He gave me a new *windshield*. I *see* it every day, and I am filled with joy.

When you're scratched deep, let Him buff away the divots.

~ *Barb Suiter*

✥ 41 ✥
All Shook Up

My husband and I sat in a booth in a restaurant with our four-year-old son beside him and our two daughters beside me. Lisa, age six, sat between me and Lori, age eight. Lori sat next to the partition she could barely peek over.

Our food was delivered by the waitress, then we bowed our heads while my husband said grace. After the amen, I picked up the salad dressing bottle when I heard a man say, "What a beautiful family."

My children certainly were! They wore Sears catalog clothes, and I dressed in the finest sale clothes. My husband was naturally handsome and appealing. We smiled and began to talk. Each of the two men asked simple questions of the children who answered like well-behaved, articulate, precocious children.

My husband and I asked them where they were from and spoke the usual niceties, then the conversation ended with their again complimenting us and wishing us well on our outing. They turned their attention to each other and their food.

My family turned our attention to the food in front of us. I glanced around at my beautiful, well-mannered, special, well…about-perfect family and felt as if I were smiling all over. It was because of me that my little children were so perfect. I trained them, I dressed them. But now it was eating time.

So I grasped the salad bottle tightly, gave it quick vigorous shakes.

Then I screamed. My girls yelled.

I screamed again. My son laughed.

My husband looked like a statue with bulging eyes. There I sat with a salad dressing bottle held up as high as my head. Two little girls had splashes of yellow salad dressing across their faces and dresses. The mess had even flown over the partition to the men's table.

I apologized profusely. They assured me all was well, but I watched them pick up their napkins. I didn't look at them again. With lowered, heated face I witnessed my girls wiping off salad dressing and they began to shake. I knew what was going to happen. The same thing that happens in church. At the slightest distraction we all lower our heads, cover our mouths, our shoulders begin to shake and we almost die laughing.

Then it started. The men left, no doubt wondering how that perfect beautiful family became shaking hyenas, laughing hysterically, except for the husband who looked like he'd rather go home, get in bed, and cover his head.

The moral of the story is: If you want to impress others, make sure your top is screwed on tightly.

~ Yvonne Lehman

❧ 42 ❧
How Stupid Can You Smile?

I've done some really stupid things concerning writing and writer's conferences. If you've ever seen me at one, you'll notice I'm the one with the big, may I say it, stupid (a word that I tell my family we don't use in our home) grin on my face the entire time. Well maybe not quite the entire time if I've just gotten a rejection from a publisher. But most of the time I'm so happy to be there instead of being various people's taxi driver at home. At conference I'm just another aspiring writer wandering from class to class, gleaning all I can from all those wonderful speakers and teachers.

At one of the first writer's conferences I attended I submitted a book proposal way before the proper time. I had seen Les Stobbe when he arrived and wanted to thank him for including something I'd written in his newsletter. When I went over to introduce myself, busy man that he was, he said, "Make an appointment with me."

He probably thought that I intended to propose something when all I'd meant to do, Southern girl that I am, was say, "Hi, kind sir, pleased to make your acquaintance and thanks for putting me in your newsletter!" Since he was the expert and I was just an attendee, I thought I better do what he asked. So I signed the sheet to have an appointment with him, since by chance I had brought a book proposal with me. I will be eternally grateful to him for having the wisdom to tell me that my book would be too much work for him. Some years later I realized that particular book was probably only for my family's eyes and he in his wisdom knew it and was just saying it in a kind way.

The second stupid thing I did at Florida Christian Writers Conference was when I finally got to meet best-selling author, Jerry Jenkins. I had a friend many years back who was a traveling minister and he'd told me a story of meeting a young writer. It was a beautiful story of how he, an elderly prophet had a personal word for the man who was struggling as he waited for his book to be published. I thought he said the man's name was Jerry Jenkins but now I think it was Peter Jenkins or maybe Jerry P. Jenkins. Nevertheless, I embarrassed myself royally and then realized that they may not remember me for my writings but they will remember me for all the goof-ups I make at these conferences.

At the time of those conferences I was pretty much a lone-ranger writer. My writing mentor, Rosemary Upton, had passed away. The writer's group she hosted named Critiqueshop had disbanded and I was pushing myself to continue writing. When I went to Florida Christian Writer's Conference I would ask myself, *What am I doing here, anyway?*

Some people think I must love to write when actually at times it is pure torture. Titles come, yet nothing follows. I hadn't been able to win any of those contests that seemed so easy to enter. I couldn't afford to gamble on entry fees with those low percentage odds of getting my money back. Procrastination seemed to be my middle name. There was always something I should do first: organize at home, clean the garage, become computer savvy. I couldn't write unless all things were perfect, but at least I managed to write something to start the day with:

Procrastinating Writer's Prayer

God, you know I'm not like others who love to write. Because of You and what You're doing in my life, I am compelled to write. But I seem to procrastinate.

I want early morning quiet (all day long). Could there please be no phone interruptions today? Add to my prayer requests: no typos, no dogs barking and no kids fighting over the computer and who gets a turn next? And please, no hot flashes! I can't take the challenge of hormones and write too. Please write through me and I promise I will get it in the email. Yes, Lord, I'll send it out, first thing tomorrow. Amen.

My writing life was on hold for many years after attending that first writer's conference and then Bam, Bam, Bam! I received three scholarships in a row. Even my husband began to think what he once considered *Donna's little hobby* might be something I was called to do. I won those scholarships by entering competitions and had the time of my life on my mini-vacations away from home. Three nights and four days surrounded by my writing heroes, all you can eat salad buffets, and the beauty of Lake Yale in sunny Florida. I also joined a national writer's group to have more accountability in my life after the first group I attended disbanded.

I set goals for myself and that's led to being published in 16 book compilations and several magazines and newspapers along the way. I am finding my voice and the encouragement within myself to press on. I have been exposed to great authors like Cecil Murphey, Dr. Calvin Miller, Eva Marie Everson, Bryan Davis, Dan Walsh, Jerry Jenkins and others too countless to name. I'm open to learning from beginning writers at conferences. I have come to enjoy the journey and find pleasure in making acquaintances of all types of writers.

Knowing that there is a big smile on my face when I am amidst the writers at conferences helps me realize I am heading on the right path. I have often thought that some of the writers will remember me for my wild hair and stupid mistakes instead of for my writing, though.

I now am adding senior moments in mix, but being remembered in any way is good, right? Actually the way I want to be remembered is as someone who encourages others to press on with a big smile.

Even a stupid smile!

~ Donna Collins Tinsley

❧ 43 ❧
Wonder Who's Calling?

"Hello, Helen, how are you and Larry?" a male voice asked when I answered the phone. Hmm, the voice was familiar, but I wasn't coming up with a name. We didn't have caller ID and cell phones weren't available in our area at that time.

"We're doing great, thank you." *Be polite*, I thought. *Surely I will figure out who this is and not seem stupid.*

"Good, how about coming to our house for lunch on Sunday after church?" *Oh my, who could this be?* He sounds like Leon our neighbor. We had eaten with him and Suzie at other times.

"Yes, that will work."

"Alright, see you at the Krafts on Sunday." Oh good, he did finally give me a name and I was right about the identity of the caller. I was glad I had averted seeming stupid.

"Thank you, we will look forward to it."

After church on Sunday, we drove the 25 miles to our home, went inside to use the bathroom and drop off our Bibles. As we were ready to head out the door, the phone rang.

"Helen, we're waiting on you. Are you coming?" the same male voice asked.

"Yes, we're ready to walk down the alley to your home. See you in a couple minutes." I hurriedly hung up the phone.

We were excited to eat and visit with Leon and Suzie. It had been awhile since we had spent time with them.

"Hi, it's nice to see you," Suzie said when she opened the door. "Come in, we're getting ready to have lunch with our friends Don and Alice. Would you like to join us?"

"That's why we're here," I reminded her. "Leon called me earlier in the week and asked us to come."

"He didn't tell me, but we have plenty." Uh oh, that didn't sound right.

The lunch was nice. Leon and Suzie are wonderful hosts and have the ability to make everyone welcome. We enjoyed visiting with them. But Leon did mention, "I don't remember calling you." An uneasiness continued to creep over me. I knew something was wrong, but I couldn't figure out what had happened.

As Larry and I walked the block back home, we discussed the unusual circumstance. Did Leon actually forget that he had called me? Had I misunderstood him? Or was this the wrong couple? If that was the case, who called me?

Back at our house, I called a couple of friends to ask if they had invited us to lunch. No, they didn't know anything about it. Each one thought it was an interesting situation and asked that I tell them later how it turned out. Actually, I preferred no one knew about it. This was beginning to seem like an embarrassing nightmare.

"God," I pleaded, "Who called me? What happed today? It looks like we barged in on Leon and Suzie and evidently have stood up another couple. Please help me straighten this out."

Two hours later, the name Krofts came to me. Oh my, could it be Bob who called? We had never eaten at Bob and June's home, but they had mentioned they wanted us to come sometime. They lived only a couple miles from where we went to church. The names Krofts and Krafts did sound similar.

I called June. When she answered the phone, I asked, "June, were we supposed to be at your house for lunch today?"

"Yes, we were expecting you after church."

"Oh, I am so sorry. I misunderstood Bob when he called earlier in the week. I thought he said to come to the Krafts, who are our neighbors."

"When he called you today and you said you ready to walk down the alley, we figured there had been some mistake. It's alright, we went ahead and ate."

"Please forgive us, we never intended to stand you up. When we showed up at the Krafts and they weren't expecting us, we knew something was wrong but couldn't figure out what happened."

"Don't worry about it Helen. Maybe we can get together another time."

Too bad this situation wasn't a nightmare. Instead, because of my pride I had caused misunderstanding for two families. I don't know whether I looked stupid to them or not, but I certainly felt stupid.

Within a few days, Larry saw Leon and explained to him about the mix-up of names. He was very gracious about it and said there was no harm done.

Both couples are great examples of how to act when someone else has a moment of stupidity. They forgave, were kind about the situation, and have remained friends with us. They may have forgotten the incident, but I haven't. I learned that asking questions is not nearly as stupid as not asking, and then getting names mixed up.

~ Helen L. Hoover

❧ 44 ❧
Look for the Signs

It was a normal day just like any other, and the necessary trip to Walmart was supposed to be quick, easy, and uneventful. And it was…at least, until my daughter and I finished our shopping and headed back to the car.

Since I always try to park in the same general area — making it easy to locate my car — I was talking and not paying close attention. The sun was setting as we approached my SUV, and shadows filled the parking lot. I hit the unlock button. Normally, the light on the side mirror would come on. It didn't. I hit the button again and again. Nothing.

Hmmm. Must not be working. Need to tell hubby when we get home. With that thought pushed aside, I walked to the driver's door and started to use the keypad on the side of the car. That's when I realized my daughter was already in the passenger seat.

Duh…must have forgotten to lock the car. Not good. I made a mental note not to ever make that mistake again and climbed in behind the wheel. It was hard to put my finger on what was wrong, but something just didn't *feel* right. Before putting the key in the ignition, a strange contraption hanging from the rearview mirror caught my eye. It was covered in beads and feathers and was most definitely not in my car before we went into the store. I glanced at my daughter and she was staring at the strange "thing" too.

At the same moment, we both realized we were in the wrong car. Frantic squeals filled the air as we exited the vehicle that was parked right next to mine. They were identical…well, except for the beads and feathers. As I climbed out, I was saying something like, "Oh my gosh. I can't believe this. I hope nobody saw us. How embarrassing. Let's get out of here!"

That's when I looked up to see a group of men walking past us toward the store. They evidently found the whole scenario quite entertaining. We heard snickers and a lot of whispering. Heads were shaking back and forth, and I could imagine comments such as, "Typical women drivers. Can't even find the right car."

I was mortified and wanted to disappear.

When my daughter and I were safely in our car, she was still squealing with laughter. I was laughing too, but also thinking of all the what-ifs: What if someone had been inside that car? What if a ferocious dog had mauled us, protecting his property? What if the owner had seen us? What if the police had come by at that moment? Would we have been accused of trying to steal a car?

Seems that even in our stupidity, God was protecting us — just like he always does. *And we know that in all things God works for the good of those who love him.*

What could have been a potentially bad situation turned out to be something comical that we could look back on and share with others. Actually, God probably found it pretty comical as well.

Moral of the story: Don't make the same stupid mistake I did. Pay close attention to where you park. If the unlock-button doesn't work, that might be a sign.

Just a thought…

- Andrea Merrell

❦ 45 ❦
Riding Oatsie

I have done many foolish things throughout my life, but the one decision that stands out among all of the rest is when I tried to ride a cranky steer in order to impress boys.

When you grow up in the country, you often pass the time in ways most city folk would consider eccentric, if not downright bizarre. My sisters and I spent many blissful hours riding on the backs of sheep, participating in rotten vegetable fights, using whatever decaying vegetable might be handy (think snowball fights with no snow, and a bit more smell and mess involved). We hurled our bodies with reckless abandon from the upper barn loft down into the ground-floor haymow, and even captured ducks with the express purpose of tying ropes around their legs in order for them to pull us, comfortably perched on inflated inner-tubes, around the farm pond (it worked!).

However, every single attempt to ride the steer was unsuccessful.

For one thing, the steer named Oatsie — a food-based name chosen in light of his eventual destination of the dinner table — was notoriously bad-tempered. He would angrily snort when anyone got near him, repeatedly stamping one front hoof on the ground in order to let us know that he meant business.

For another thing, Oatsie had taken a particular dislike to me. The fact that I had been the one to care for him from birth, first bottle-feeding the tiny calf and then later feeding him choice bits of greenery, had initially resulted in an apparent fondness of the calf for me. Unfortunately, I was also the person who ensured that he would be a steer and not a bull, so any positive association that I might have had instantaneously evaporated.

Although Oatsie would not go out of his way to interact with any other person, he would usually just leave them alone. I was a different case, though. When he saw me inside the pen, Oatsie would flank me, and either try to smash me against the barn's exterior or (his preferred approach) trap me between his massive body and the electric fence, causing me to experience all of the joys of prolonged contact with the fence. Although I made several attempts at riding Oatsie, I had not once been successful.

Although I would have been happy to let it go at that, my sisters were not as content. One day, when friends of our family who had teenaged boys the same ages as my sisters and me, came over for a visit, *it* happened.

My middle sister, a self-avowed expert at eliciting reactions from her siblings, somehow managed to get me agree to ride Oatsie in order to impress the boys. Despite the fact that I knew that any attempt to get near the steer, never mind actually ride him, would likely end in disaster, I approached the steer with trepidation while the others held him still.

Oatsie was angry. His eyes rolled back into his head — a sure sign to anyone who knew anything about cattle that he was one infuriated steer. His hide shuddered as if a million biting ants were attacking, and his tail swished violently from side to side, lashing the ones attempting to hold his hind quarters still.

Somehow — to this day, I honestly cannot remember how I did it — I made it up on Oatsie's back and readied myself for the ride ahead, mentally rifling through the (sadly) limited amount of bull-riding-related information lodged somewhere in the far recesses of my brain.

My middle sister was to count down from ten, and I readied myself for the ride of my life. When she reached one, everyone let go of Oatsie and quickly jumped back so they would not inadvertently be trampled by the irate steer.

Unable to jump to safety, I squeezed my knees as tightly against Oatsie's massive bulk as my trembling legs could possibly manage and wrapped my arms around his thick neck. I pressed the side of my face firmly against the back of his head, determined to stay on his back at least long enough to not shame myself in front of everyone.

The minute that everyone let go of the steer, my youngest sister slapped Oatsie firmly on the hind quarters and yelled at the top of her lungs. This, of course, did not endear him to me and he took off like a shot, bucking his offended hind end high into the air.

Although I did make the requisite nine seconds for bull riding sans rope or other helpful equipment, my short thrill of success was abruptly halted when one particularly exuberant spin-and-buck combination (coupled with a bovine snort of wrathful glee) caused my body to launch in an ungraceful parabola of doom, landing even less gracefully, belly first, into a giant pile of soggy manure with a loud, juicy, splat.

As soon as I was capable of breathing again, words more filthy than the substance which was then encrusting my body spewed forth from my mouth, primarily discussing what I would do to my youngest sibling once I reached her. I then launched myself from my fecal cocoon, pursuing my youngest sister with abandon fueled by a fiery fury.

Later, I learned that one of the teen boys recorded the entire event. This was unfortunate not only due to the fact that my humiliating launch into the manure pile had been recorded for all perpetuity, but that my parents heard my threats toward my youngest sister, validating her whiny claims of older-sister-maltreatment.

So, at the end of it all, I ended up in hot water (literally and figuratively!), was given my youngest sister's chores as a consequence for my (justifiably, at least I thought) angrily-spoken words, was the star of a rather popular (and horribly embarrassing) video snippet, was the recipient of massively large amounts of ridicule by teenage boys, had to live with my smugly smirking sisters who were reveling in their (temporary) superiority, and am now known, for the remainder of my life, as "the girl who landed in poo."

On reminiscing about this event, one verse has come to my mind: Pride goes before destruction, and a haughty spirit before a fall (Proverbs 16:18). Somehow, I never thought I would ever experience such a literal interpretation of Scripture.

~ *Marybeth Mitcham*

~ 46 ~
Filled to the Measure

My stomach growled, and my eyes searched for a clock, as if needing to confirm the body's signal for hunger. The clock, strategically hung over a snack machine, confirmed that I'd missed lunch. As I sat there in the waiting room of the full-service car wash, I glanced out the window where soap suds and water were flying, and all thoughts of counting points for my diet washed right out of my brain.

I knew better. I'd been taught HALT, the acronym for Hungry, Angry, Lonely, Tired — conditions that leave us vulnerable to temptation. But five hours had passed since my skimpy breakfast of a mini-bagel, and H had taken control of my brain.

From that moment on, I operated on autopilot. Pick up purse from floor; pull out wallet, open change compartment, dig out quarters, walk over to snack machine. My eyes settled on a bag of baked cheese crackers and I rationalized, *those aren't so bad.* But with quarters ready to slide into the slot, my eyes slid down — to the Nabs. In Weight Watchers, one pack of Nabs counts five points — which is equivalent to a whole meal.

Those Nabs were good.

I washed them down with Diet Coke. *No harm done, that will be my lunch.*

However, when I returned home, I found myself in the kitchen foraging for food. I opened a cabinet. *Hmm, think I'll have a cookie.* Munch. Munch.

Those chips look pretty good. Crunch. Crunch. Crunch.

Whoa! Sanity returned and I realized I'd certainly put more than enough calories into my body. *So why am I still hungry?* I looked at the cookies and chips in the cabinet. *Because I've filled my body with junk!* I finally poured healthy cereal into a bowl, and covered it with skim milk. I sat down at the kitchen table, ate the cereal, and felt nourishment flow throughout my body. Whew, finally contentment.

I've found the same thing is true of our souls. Many times we try to fill them with junk by eating or starving ourselves, sleeping or being a workaholic, making money or being a shopaholic. We may turn to drugs or alcohol, or even try to dull our senses with television or the internet. But none of these satisfy, and any of these things in excess can end up hurting us.

Our souls were designed to be filled only with Christ. When we allow him to fill us, he gives us the power to let go of destructive things, and to find peace that comes only from our souls being filled to the measure with the fullness of God — and we are finally free to experience true contentment.

- Susan Dollyhigh

47
Bubba
and the Bachelorette Party

To say I am an over achiever may be an understatement. When I get an idea in my head I just can't rest until I see it through. Most times I consider it a blessing. Then there was the brainstorm of an idea that left me questioning my judgment.

My youngest daughter's bachelorette party was to be held at my house. I was pleased to be able to host the party. The festivities included a Mexican meal and margaritas.

I wanted to leave a lasting memory of a great time that night and came up with the ultimate party pleaser, a male stripper — not your expected gorgeous hunk of a guy who walks through the door as a policeman and peels off his uniform leaving nothing to the imagination. I didn't want anything like that. What I was looking for was something comedic, definitely not erotic.

I had visions of a guy showing up and being a showstopper and bringing giggles. A comedy skit would be an added treat for female friends and family members celebrating with the bride-to-be. What I got was Bubba, who turned out to be a bachelorette party's biggest nightmare. I hired Bubba, who was supposed to make a surprise entrance under the pretense that he was my daughter's long lost boyfriend.

The night of the party I was on pins and needles awaiting Bubba's arrival. When he showed up, the bottom began to fall out of my planned surprise. Prior to the night of the party this guy called and asked for some pertinent information about the bride-to-be, like: where she hung out after school, what kind of car she drove in high school, and a few funny things she did in her younger years. That would personalize the comedy skit and leave the guests in stitches. He would end the hilarity by stripping down to a wrestling outfit.

But before Bubba reached for the first button on his patched and torn flannel shirt, my daughter was long gone.

I followed close behind as she ran right out the front door.

As she sat on the porch steps crying and asking how I could do this to her, my eldest daughter came to my defense. She told her sister that she, too, had thought Bubba would be a funny addition to the party.

Then my oldest said something that caught me off guard. She shook her head and said, matter of factly, "I knew we should have gone with the midget!"

What!

That would have made me laugh if I hadn't been on the verge of tears. The comment further irritated her younger sister.

Looking back, I should have known that Bubba would be a bust. His shtick was supposed to have been that of a hillbilly. The only trouble was, when I met him at the door and saw his unkempt appearance, it was clear that he was not *portraying* a hillbilly. His gray hair foretold the tale that he was more like grandfather material — not at all even remotely believable as my daughter's past love.

Against my better judgment I did let him into my home, even though he had spent a good portion of his time memorizing his lines out in our gangway, telling me to get out of his space when I went to check on him.

So it was that Bubba stormed through the door, reciting his generic shtick, oblivious to my daughter's look of pure disdain. Every bit of information I gave him about her past he flubbed up, from what high school she attended to what kind of car she drove.

My daughter was mortified at being put on the spot while enduring such a pitiful performance, I felt like crawling into a hole and never coming out.

Although I am proud of having a reputation for going all out when planning special occasions, now I have to accept that I'd gone too far. Instead of enhancing the festivities I fell miserably short. Somehow, trying to console myself that I had the best of intentions just didn't cut it.

My loving husband and best friend tell me to quit beating myself up about this, but it's not easy while memories of Bubba are still on the brain.

Someday we may look back at this together and laugh. It may take awhile though. Bubba was a buffoon whose act was sickening, not side splitting.

On the heels of my daughter's wedding I'm laying low. This mother of the bride is not planning any more surprises for her daughter.

I think I'll reserve my party planning to what I know best — tending to the food and ambiance of the occasion.

Some day we just may laugh at this. Some day she may see the humor when retelling the memory. And, by then, I hope she won't be too hard on me.

~ Kathy Whirity

~ 48 ~
Indecent Exposure

I looked down at the doll cake I had set on the floor of my husband's old pickup truck for the ride home from the bakery. The jostling over the bumpy country roads, and my driving at faster than normal speeds, had caused the frosting bodice of the fashion doll's evening gown to slide down around her waist, leaving her bare bosomed. The nine-year-old girls coming to Tina's birthday party in the morning would have plenty to say about that.

I thought I could wrap a few rows of ribbon around her chest and hide her indecency. Only Tina and I would know. I hadn't planned to drive the old beater, but honestly, had forgotten about picking up the cake, so I had not included it on my To-Do list. When the bakery called with my reminder, there was no time to go home and get the car. I had not arranged for anyone to pick the children up after school. I could not be late getting to their bus stop.

If you looked up "multitasking mom" in the dictionary you would find my picture. I worked off lists, freeing my brain cells from life's minutia and saving them for the momentous things. My ducks were in a row and I had learned to keep them that way out of necessity. In fact, I had taught a few Organizing-Your-Life workshops for women.

My two children were in elementary school: Tina in third grade, Kurtis in first grade. Kurtis was disabled and had doctor or therapy appointments four days a week. I had begun working on my bachelor's degree at the nearest state college, a 50-mile commute in one direction. I was enrolled in 21 units and working three part-time jobs in order to pay for my education, child care and commute costs. I carried a grade point average good enough to allow me to eventually graduate with highest honors. I prided myself on never saying, "Don't bother me, I'm doing homework," to my children. I planned for every minute of my day and used every minute as planned. Picking up that cake was what threw the day off kilter — or was it Annie?

My flow chart for the evening activities was working effectively, but I could feel the stress of being behind schedule. Our young Boston terrier, Annie, was let outside to take care of business after being in all day. The children were settled in to after school endeavors. I put steaks under the broiler so dinner would be ready when my husband came home from work. Since we had four tickets to the local community theater I went to take a quick shower. I started the water running, but before I was able to get into the shower, I heard Annie barking in an unusual way.

"Tina, please go check on Annie. See why she is barking," I called out while beginning to undress. We lived on a four-acre rural parcel of land in the country with horses, goats and other livestock. We had neighbors, but trees and out-buildings kept us from being visible to each other.

"Mom, Annie is caught in the barbed-wire!"

Tina and I ran down the hall and out the back door, to where I could see Annie's little black and white body swinging from the second strand of barbed wire fencing. The skin on her neck had stuck on a barb as she jumped between the strands. Kurtis, slowed by his disabilities and leg brace, arrived at the scene after we did. I supported the frantic Annie with one hand while trying to free her entangled flesh from the barbs with my other hand. The longer I worked the more her black eyes bugged out in frightened panic. She began gnawing on my fingers until the blood dripped from them and I could not tell her blood from my own. None of my soothing words worked on this terrified little canine. I needed help.

Thinking about which of my neighbors would be home at 5:00 p.m and the abilities of my children, I sent them out. "Tina, go down the hill and tell Brenda I need help. Annie is stuck in the fence. Kurtis, go next door and tell John I need help. Annie is stuck in the fence."

Now all I had to do was support Annie's 12 pounds of weight to keep her from further harming herself until help arrived.

Five minutes later I looked up to see Brenda, her husband John, and teenage son, also John, the next door neighbor and my children rounding the corner of our house. I guess it was something about the way they all looked at me that made me realize for the first time, I had run out of the house wearing only the underwear I had put on that morning — the same bra and panties I had been wearing since before I lost 87 pounds dieting — the same bra and panties that should have been thrown away months earlier — the same underwear I should have died of embarrassment in right then and there.

These were good neighbors. John walked up and with one snip of the wire cutters he carried in his hands Annie was free of the barbed wire. All three of the men turned and walked away without uttering a word or sputtering a laugh within range of my hearing. Brenda came inside to help me tend to Annie and my wounds.

Things had not been going well inside either. Brenda first had to press the reset button on the blaring smoke detector, turn on the fan over the stove, open the windows to clear the house of smoke, remove the charcoaled steaks from the broiler and turn off the now cold water running in the shower. When my husband walked in, Brenda walked out. "We've had a few problems here," was all she said to him.

I had already come up with a new dinner plan; one I was sure would please the kids. I knew we could stop at the supermarket and buy a new birthday cake on the way home from the play, and it would take care of the bare bosomed doll issue as well, so I was prepared when my husband, insensitive to my distress, noticed the way overdone steaks and asked, "What's for dinner?"

"Well, underneath the frosting of that doll's skirt is carrot cake." I set the knife, four forks and small plates on the table.

Everyone hoped I wasn't kidding.

~ *Mason K. Brown*

～ 49 ～
And You Teach What?

The auditorium seated several hundred people and from my folding chair on the stage, it looked filled to capacity. The first parent information night always drew a big crowd; the succeeding ones, not so much, but the teachers and staff were used to that. I was used to it, too, already boasting five "deployments" under my belt. I was a veteran — blasé and confident. In the 10 or so minutes allotted me, I would captivate and entertain my audience. My drama background would ensure I had plenty of witty quips and clever observations about middle school students in general that would engender thundering, appreciative applause.

Therein lies the problem.

I was more than blasé. I was extremely and disgustingly smug. Sassy would be the word I'd use if it were one of my seventh graders. Forget all the scripture verses about pride coming before falling flat on your face, or pride, leading to disgrace. When the principal introduced me, I was just short of levitating from my chair. I sashayed to the podium, set my notes down and beamed out at my beloved spectators.

"Good evening. What a wonderful turnout. This promises to be an exciting and rewarding year, and I know your children are primed and raring to get at it." (chuckles and nods and assorted smiles) "As you know, I will be teaching sixth, seventh and eighth grade—"

At that precise moment, the earth ceased spinning on its axis. I glanced at my notes, which suddenly turned into Mandarin Chinese and swallowed. The back of my neck itched and I longed to scratch. Hands gripping the sides of the podium, I stared out at a sea of expectant faces, waiting for me to finish my sentence. *Yes, yes, you will be teaching sixth, seventh and eighth grade… what? Go on. You will be teaching…*

I swallowed again. The itch at the back of my neck morphed into a tingling that danced across my face. Even worse, a deep, searing heat suddenly rose up from heaven-knew-where and flooded neck, cheeks and ears — ears that were by no means small and fearfully visible, due to my short hair. The urge to flee took center stage and my podium grip tightened.

"As I was saying," I coughed to buy time. "I will be teaching sixth, seventh and eighth grade—" I brushed non-existent hairs off my forehead "— sixth, seventh and eighth grade, uh…"

"Language arts," someone hissed from the row of chairs behind me.

To say relief flooded over my body would be more than a cliché. Relief deluged and cascaded over me and I almost sang a high C note. Thank goodness the drama background took over and I merely inhaled, exhaled, and calmly said, "Language arts. Sixth, seventh and eighth grade language arts. I will also be offering a drama club after school, where we hope to write, direct and produce original plays."

A few more pertinent facts were added, and then I snapped my notes together, offered another smile and nod and resumed my chair, weak from the passing adrenalin surge. One more stupid moment to add to my repertoire. What was that verse, again, about excessive arrogance and pride?

~ *Theresa Jenner Garrido*

50
The Wrong Garden

After several busy days of co-hosting a tour of Israel, I looked forward to quiet time at the grounds of the Garden Tomb. Away from the noise and hustle of the city, I would be able to spend time alone with God and write.

From our hotel, my husband Alan and I walked to the walls of the Garden. He wanted to roam the narrow streets of the Old City so he left me and continued his journey. We decided he would stop to pick me up on his way back.

The doors in the long wall were closed so I waited for them to open. Finally, a man approached and started to enter. I explained I wanted to find a spot to sit and meditate.

Without speaking, he motioned for me to follow him. After we were inside the grounds, he pointed to a bench under a tree and left.

Even though I had been to the Garden Tomb several times, nothing looked familiar. I didn't see the winding walkways through the garden, the extensive flowers and foliage or the tomb cut from the rock.

A gravel drive was beside my bench. Cars parked near a building I had never noticed on previous trips. A few people went in and out, but I saw no tourists.

Walls surrounding the garden muffled blaring city noises. In my quiet spot, I escaped the busyness of our tour and prayed. Birds sang while I wrote. The serenity under a shady tree offered peace to a tired pilgrim.

After a while, I decided to explore the unfamiliar part of the Garden Tomb. Just off a dirt path a tall wall surrounded a courtyard. I strolled inside and discovered a stone church.

When I saw nuns in the area, I realized I had mistakenly entered the grounds of a Catholic church instead of the Garden Tomb. However, my curiosity urged me to continue exploring.

Cautiously, I pushed open the huge, wooden door and hoped I wouldn't interrupt a worship service. A magnificent, marble sanctuary welcomed me. Towering pink and white striped marble arches and columns created grandeur in the tranquil church.

Sunlight streamed through exquisite, high stained glass windows which lined both sides of the empty chapel.

Beneath the windows, marble arches formed small galleries. I studied the paintings of saints that hung in each enclosure.

Carrying a bucket of water in her hand, a nun entered the church and began silently cleaning the pews, benches, and shelves. She smiled at me but kept working. Her quiet service was an inspiration to me.

Three gigantic paintings hung near the altar. In the center one, Jesus extended one hand in welcome to me and clutched the Scriptures with the other. His eyes held mine.

What I thought was a stupid mistake in going to the wrong place, wasn't a mistake at all. Jesus welcomed me to the oasis of peace and tranquility in the midst of the hectic city.

Neither the man, who kindly offered me a place to retreat, nor the nun, who smiled at me, made me feel uncomfortable at my mistake. Both displayed a servant's heart and reminded me to serve as though to Jesus.

My morning of refreshment gave me strength, encouragement, and inspiration to continue serving. How thankful I was for my mistake which was God's plan.

> "I know the plans I have for you," declares the Lord, "plans to prosper you and not to harm you, plans to give you hope and a future. Then you will call upon me and come and pray to me, and I will listen to you. You will seek me and find me when you seek me with all your heart."
>
> Jeremiah 29:11–13 NIV

~ Rebecca Carpenter

51
Crash Landing

Swish. Thud. I landed in an awkward heap at the bottom of the banister rail I had been foolish enough to slide down.

A concerned male voice roused me from checking to see if I was still in one piece. "Ma'am, are you hurt?

The word *ma'am* conjured up images of southern plantations, hoopskirts, and Scarlett O'Hara. I stopped rubbing my elbow and looked up. And up. Past over-sized shoes to six feet of rugged good looks topped by sandy hair and concerned blue eyes.

Speechless, I gulped. The young man I had claimed for my own weeks earlier towered above me.

They say when in danger your whole life flashes through your mind. Humiliation and a skinned elbow produced similar results. Sprawled at the stranger's feet, the past month's events ran through my brain like our local rivers in full flood…

I lived in a town so small that city people thought our zip code was A-E-I-O-U. Transfer students were always an event. So news about a new football-playing Junior spread like wildfire, especially among the girls determined to "set their caps" for him, as our grandmothers used to say. Our town loved sports. Fans turned out *en masse* for home games. The exodus to away games looked like a scene from *Hoosiers*.

As a student office girl one period each day, I knew all about incoming students. I soon received dozens of inquiries from others, especially the girls, but merely replied, "I really can't say." (I didn't explain whether it was because I didn't know or wouldn't say because of confidentiality.) I also secretly rejoiced. The privileged information gave me an advantage. So did the fact that Jack's mother, a long-time acquaintance of my parents, was going to teach fourth grade, along with my mother.

"He's mine!" I exulted. "All mine."

Joy gave way to reality. I was fairly attractive but so were many of my friends. How could I make an impression the new boy strong enough to girl-proof him against a flock of eager contenders for his attention?

Well, Mom had taught me the first step to achievement is believing something is possible. Each time I thought of the new boy I silently repeated, *He's mine.*

One morning the desk telephone rang. (No cell phones back then. No intercom.) My principal/boss had gone to the far end of the building earlier, but told me to come get him when the call came in. I hurried into the hall from our second floor office. The banister rail offered the fastest way down the steep flight of stairs to the entrance level. I gathered my full, flowered skirt around me. Down I went.

Swish. Thud. I landed at the bottom and looked up. Oh, dear. A few inches more and I'd have knocked the good-looking stranger out the still-open front door!

"Ma'am, are you hurt?" the boy repeated.

I rubbed my elbow. "N-not really." I took his outstretched hand and scrambled to my feet. "Thanks. I have to go find the principal."

Scuttled is the only word that describes my embarrassed retreat. So much for making a first impression. I dropped Jack's strong hand and turned toward the short flight of stairs to the basement. As I rounded them I heard him chuckle, then call, "I never dreamed I'd have such great luck. My first day here and the prettiest girl in school falls for me!"

After I recovered from my humiliating experience, Jack and I became good friends. We even dated now and then.

But never again did I slide down that banister rail.

~ Colleen L. Reece

~ 52 ~
Gee, I Wish I Could Get Tired

After months of prayer, asking God to show me what I should do after graduation from Taylor University, I knew I was to return to the mountains of western North Carolina. I asked for biblical confirmation that I should become a teacher and coach, and minister to teens about how Jesus Christ would change their lives if they trusted him.

I was given many indications but the condensed version is that I opened the scriptures to 1 Timothy 4:11–16, and read that one should not be looked down upon because of being young. Instruction was given about being an example in speech, conduct, love, faith, and purity by keeping a close watch on one's self while teaching and to stay true to what is right.

I now know that God desired for me to share the Gospel with students in the classroom, on the athletic fields, in after-school activities and in creative ways outside the classroom.

One of those opportunities would be to create a replica of Wandering Wheels bicycling ministry, formed by Bob Davenport, a former UCLA All-American running back and the Head Football Coach of Taylor University. Coach wanted to challenge students that Jesus Christ was sufficient for all their needs by riding a bicycle across America, in which I had previously been involved. My experience included two long-distance trips. One was a 1,200-mile trip around the coast of Florida. The other was a 2,800-mile tour through seven European countries.

My planned trip with teens would challenge young men and women physically, mentally, socially and spiritually. This would be achieved by peddling a ten-speed bicycle hundreds of miles a day, trusting God moment-by-moment as they competed for space with 16-wheelers on America's highways while sharing Christ through words and songs. At that time a popular song was "Good Vibrations" by the Beach Boys. My thought was that we would call ourselves Rolling Vibrations — a bicycling touring company who witnessed to others through music.

Finally, the teens and I began our first trip. We would bicycle through southeastern states in less than three weeks. The riders often peddled over 150 miles in one day. One day was extremely difficult as we battled heavy rain, strong headwinds and crowded highways. I quickly learned that truck drivers don't like to compete with 30 to 40 bicyclists on two lane highways, although we rode in groups of six, spread out by several miles. We stayed on the small white line on the edge of the road but many times were run off the road.

To make matters worse an electrical storm forced us to wait three hours and ride as the sun was setting. We got in late, literally exhausted. Many riders were so tired they fell asleep without eating or taking a shower.

The next morning we arose early and headed to a Shriner's hospital where we were scheduled to entertain recovering children. We wheeled kids in wheelchairs, beds, and cots into the auditorium. Some had never walked. Many wore braces or used crutches.

One of my football players, James Campbell, called "Smokey" came up to me before we performed and said, "Coach, I can't do this anymore. I am too tired. I'm beginning to hate that stupid bicycle. I can't do it. I am just too tired."

At that moment the little boy in the wheel chair that Smokey was pushing looked up at this massive, well-conditioned gifted black athlete and said, "Gee, Mr. Smokey, I'd give anything…Anything!…if I could get tired. Even if it was only for a minute."

Smokey and I looked down at the boy and became teary eyed. We all three hugged each other as the little guy said, "Smokey, you get on that bicycle. I know you can do it. I know you can."

Later in the morning we shared that story during our farewell performance. The director of the hospital said it was one of the most inspirational things that had ever happened there and everyone was talking about us. We said thank you but he was greatly mistaken. Those children were the ones who were inspirational and changed our lives that day.

A few miles down the road I pulled up beside Smokey and asked how he was doing today. He flashed that huge smile and said, "I'm doing ok, coach."

He paused and looked at me in silence for a moment and then said, "I am really glad you asked me to come on this trip. I'll be honest. I hate this stupid bicycle but this trip is changing my life. Thanks, coach."

It's amazing to me what God can do when we allow him to. In an age where there are planes that fly faster than the speed of sound, God used a stupid bicycle to change a young man's life. In a society that worships physical fitness and praises athletes to nearly the level of a deity, God used a paralyzed eight-year-old boy to change a gifted athlete's perspective on gratefulness. Who knows, maybe that same God has plans to use you and me to change others' lives around the world? Let's give Him a chance.

~ Tommy Scott Gilmore, III

❧ 53 ❧
A Twisted Kiss

The kitchen looked and smelled like Thanksgiving. Supplies for fresh cranberry relish, stuffing, and pumpkin pies covered the kitchen counter. I had a special blessing to be thankful for. My sister, Loucretia, was still tucked in bed. I was pleased that she was resting. The past year had been an awful one for her. Her job in the world of finance turned sour when the market crashed, which resulted in a job change and loss of steady income.

I knew relaxation, family time, and comfort food was what she needed to revive her spirit. I whisked my car keys off the hook, grabbed my purse and looked forward to the evening. By five o'clock I would have returned from school where I worked. I'd be tearing bread into chunks for stuffing and chatting with my sister. My son and nephew would be playing and my daughter would be on her way home from college.

With those thoughts in mind, I tiptoed to the garage, started the car ignition, used the remote to raise the door, and pulled out into the crisp November air.

As I pulled out, the car jolted, accompanied by the crunch of metal. I turned to look over my shoulder and saw my car's right rear smacked into the left front side of my sister's car. The collision had the look of a twisted kiss — but a gargantuan one, to say the least. My stomach turned into a sea of acid.

I pulled the car forward, stopped the motor, and walked around to survey the damage. My car had a gash on the side. But Loucretia's looked like a tank had backed into it. The front grill was smashed, the headlight hung down like a wobbling eyeball, and the driver's door was bent.

I was sick to my stomach, but I snapped several photographs before getting back into my car to rush to work. Instead of waking my sister, I'd decided to contact my husband from the school, get my students settled, and come back home to wake Loucretia.

When I arrived at school, I opened my phone. On it was a text from my husband. "Good morning. Watch out for Loucretia's car, you aren't blocked in but it would be very easy to crash into."

I texted a reply. "I just hit it. Didn't see message."

"Very funny," he texted, then apparently reconsidered. "No judgment from me, my record is terrible."

"I'm traumatized. Maybe I should call her."

"You didn't leave a note?"

"No! Ha. Calling insurance now. I'll text her."

His wisdom alerted me. "You may have to walk her into it more gently than a text."

My first graders' voices were getting loud. My frustration with myself grew. "Sorry, I can't text anymore."

I settled my class, then dialed the insurance company. As soon as the insurance agent answer, I tiptoed into the conversation. "I'd like to report an accident."

"Are you safe? Do you need assistance?"

"Yes, I'm safe and yes, I need assistance." I paused. "No one is hurt. I hit a car in my driveway."

"Let me guess. You have company for Thanksgiving."

I sighed. "Yes, and it's my sister's car."

"Okay, I'll need your sister's phone number and —"

"Wait. Don't call her yet. She's still sleeping."

He laughed. "She doesn't know?"

"Not yet." The conversation continued. Finally, the agent told me to send the images to him and he'd access the damage.

"Thank you. I'm going to go back home and wake up my sister."

"Good luck with that." The insurance agent chuckled again. "Have your sister call this number as soon as you can."

"Thanks." I arranged for my class to be supervised, and then drove home.

My stomach sunk to my feet as I walked to the bedroom. "Loucretia, wake up." She rolled over and yawned. "Sorry, Loucretia, I bumped into your car on the way to work."

She bolted out of bed, pulled on shoes and a coat.

"I'm so sorry," I cried. Every wrong thing in her life had played through my mind like a movie. That last thing she needed was another financial mess.

Taking the blame, she said, "I thought I parked far enough away."

But I was to blame. "I never look behind me in the driveway. No one is ever parked here."

Loucretia started laughing. "No worries, Terri."

I wasn't so sure. "The insurance company needs to talk to you right away."

Within the next few hours, my husband suggested I ask our neighbor, who worked on damaged cars as a side business, to check the cars. The insurance company called with an estimate to correct my stupidity.

Before the Thanksgiving holiday was over, my neighbor had graciously fixed Loucretia's car. We paid our neighbor and skipped filing an insurance claim. My husband wrote my sister a check based on the insurance estimate.

We had a wonderful Thanksgiving. Afterwards, she drove home with an unblemished car and money in her pocket. And I had proof that God takes even a stupid moment and redeems it.

- Terri Kelly

54
Repeat After Me: I Am Not the Holy Spirit

They were in a bitter battle.
Three families.
Three perspectives.
Three sets of strong emotions.
There were moments when it appeared the fight might be ending, a lull so-to-speak. Just when it seemed they would make amends and agree to disagree, something or someone would explode.

These three families were a part of the body of Christ, the local church. I was their pastor's wife, in my mid-twenties and they were all a decade or more older than me.

I witnessed the bickering as it began to poison our sweet congregation and yet, there was nothing I could do.

Almost nothing…

I read the beautiful story of Corrie ten Boom; how she was able to forgive the men who murdered her family and stole all but her life. I read her words as she recalled the moment she visited a congregation and looked into the face of the man who murdered her dear sister. She chose to forgive him.

If God could help Corrie forgive such horrendous pain and crime, God could help these families find healing through forgiving one another.

And then I acted.

I typed that story, made three copies, folded them and addressed the envelopes. Without a word to my pastor husband, the letters were mailed. A surge of satisfaction washed over me as I imagined each family opening the letter, reading it and rereading it. I smiled to myself as I pictured each one breaking down in a heap of, "Forgive us Lord." I patted myself on the back as I envisioned the families would meet, talk, pray, hug, and all would be right in the world.

Did I mention I did not sign the letters?

I went my way and didn't think of it again. Well…I wouldn't have thought of it again…if…

A few days later, after running errands, I walked into my husband's office to let him know I was home. He had no color in his face as he sat, glassy eyed, staring at the wall.

"You're not going to believe it," he said. "Someone has anonymously sent letters to all three of the feuding families. The letters are copies of a Corrie ten Boom story about forgiveness. Mr. Justified called first. He is angry. Later a call came from Mrs. Vinegar and she is fuming."

I entered a suspended state of being, swallowing and waiting to hear how this was going to end.

"Mr. You-Better-Fix-This called just a few minutes ago. He's planning to have the envelope analyzed. He might press charges. They are all blaming each other for the letter. I never would have believed it could get worse. But it got worse."

"Uh…I, uh…I s-s-sent the letters."

He sat there and stared at me like he didn't hear me. I waited, feeling somewhat like a teenager who had been caught out past curfew.

"What should I do? I'm sorry. I just wanted to help. I thought it would help."

"You're going to have to go, house to house, and let them know the letters came from you. You can't talk to them over the phone. You need to go tonight, meet with them face to face and explain. Maybe they will calm down."

Praying and begging God to fix this mess I had created, I made my way to the first home.

Mr. Justified and his wife answered the door together and invited me in. I wasn't sure how I should approach the confession of my offense. So I cried. And I stumbled over every word. And they were kind and forgiving.

Feeling somewhat fortified by the positive result, I headed over to the home of Mr. You-Better-Fix-This and his wife.

Enter. Sit. Replay. Cry. Stumble. Anger. Anger. Anger. A little bit of yelling and some more anger.

Whatever strength I had gained from the first stop had been washed away by the shame I experienced at the second. Acid indigestion set in and my head hurt. I left that home with no forgiveness for what I had done.

Two down and one to go.

Mrs. Vinegar and her husband were glad to see me. I didn't quite cry this time; it was more like sniffles. Several tissues later, Mrs. Vinegar informed me it would have been okay had I just signed my name. They were not as kind as the folks at my first stop but not as cruel as the second. All in all, I had done what I could to correct my wrong.

I needed to make one more forgiveness stop. To my husband. He was still at his desk. There was a bit more color in his face. I explained that I never meant to cause him trouble, that I had always hoped to be the pastor's wife that supported ministry.

He was understanding and forgiving and thankful the snowball effect of anonymous mail had come to a stop.

As time went on, the issues resolved themselves.

What I learned that evening has helped me to this day, almost 25 years later.

The moral of this story has two parts.

One: If I can't sign my name I shall not send a letter.

Two: I am not the Holy Spirit.

~ Shelley Pierce

Love Those Typos

When reading over a scene I had written,
two character friends are eating grilled chicken sandwiches and French fries.
I had typed,
"She dipped a fly in her ketchup."

~ Yvonne

~ 55 ~
Lawn 911

My husband, Ken, and I purchased a home in a rural area in 2005 to get away from the city noise, traffic, and the confining space of the subdivision we were in. We wanted a house in an area where we couldn't watch our neighbors' television from our yard.

After we moved, a riding lawn mower became a necessity. All our previous residences had been graced with yards small enough to use a push mower. We now owned three acres of grass, which I referred to as my three-acre estate. My husband named our ground Hoggy Acres; not because we raise pigs, but because he rides a Harley motorcycle.

A trip to the local home supply store left us several hundred dollars lighter and the owners of a new machine. This new toy was babied, washed, driven even when the grass didn't need to be cut, and put away in the garage out of the weather. Lawn maintenance rivaled an adventure a theme park would envy.

A few months later, Ken was sent overseas to work. Our sons were both grown and had left home years before, so now I was the sole caretaker of our little estate. That meant I had to eiher learn how to operate all the equipment for lawn care or pay someone else to do the chore.

I decided to learn.

My lesson progressed well and I graduated with honors while Ken watched me perform the grass clipping task. After he shipped out I stayed busy and kept our yard maintained and beautiful. I rejoiced when I learned to use the weed eater and zipped away those weeds with such gusto a landscape artist would be proud.

The summer weeks extended into months and I continued to ride what I now called my "little tractor," plowing through grass like an expert. I manhandled the gas can, filling the tank when needed, and cleaned my lawn machine before I put her away each time I finished my work.

One Saturday in late summer, as it was time to complete the job again, I got the mower out and started it. I surveyed the land and wondered how grass could grow so fast and how the yard could have gained at least an acre since we moved in.

Tractor and I were rolling along nicely when clanging noises started coming from the engine.

Hmm, I wonder what that is. The machine kept running so I kept going, around trees, along the edge of the back porch, and into the center of the back yard.

Screech, grind, ping, clunk, pop! This time she died. And didn't revive no matter how many times I turned the key. I looked around and discovered I was at the end of the yard and even though the two and one-half acres that comprised the back yard separated me from the garage, it looked as though it were miles. My home looked like a dollhouse from that distance.

I knew I couldn't push this beast (she wasn't my tractor anymore, she now had a new name) all the way back to the garage, so I traversed next door to garner some help. After my neighbor walked to where I had become stranded, he looked the machine over, turned the key and said, "When was the last time you put oil in this?"

Uh-oh.

"Well…never," I replied with my head down. The red on my face from the heat now escalated to embarrassment as I had to admit my stupidity. He didn't say anything, but I imagine he was thinking *dumb woman.*

"Is there a Lawn 911?" I asked.

He looked at the machine, then back at me. "I think you better call the mortuary."

I stood in the center of my three acres of grass and stared in disbelief at the pile of now useless junk. I'd destroyed a couple of thousand dollars' worth of equipment because of carelessness. I knew oil needed to be changed, but I didn't think about *adding.*

My next task was to tell Ken that the precious dweller of his man-cave-garage had received last rites in the middle of the yard…and we would have to fork over more money to purchase another one. He was understanding, as always, and blamed himself for not telling me to check the oil often. I think I was more absorbed in listening to the directions he gave about working the thing than in maintaining it. Nevertheless, we can now laugh about my yard antics.

His return from overseas put the lawn care back on him, although I do help occasionally. We became double mower owners, and I have lubrication down to a science now. When he starts the engine, I can be heard to yell over the roar, "Did you check the oil?"

At least I can really say, "I'll never make that mistake again."

My lawnmower stopped working from lack of oil. I didn't maintain. If I don't operate my life in daily maintenance with the word of God I become dry and lifeless. But filling my reservoir with the oil of the Holy Spirit fuels my soul with His love, joy, peace, patience, kindness, goodness, faithfulness, gentleness, and self-control. My life won't get stuck when I am full of His oil.

~ Barbara Latta

~ 56 ~
Maps Don't Trump a Sense of Direction

I was born without a sense of direction.

It's hard to admit that I'm a directionless individual but it's true. Everything's fine if I know the way to and from a place.

That doesn't save me in the case of detours.

One fall evening in the pre-cell-phone era, after visiting my brother at a hospital I realized there were detour signs leading from the parking lot.

I panicked.

The parking attendant knew how to get to the highway, but she lost me after gesturing for two right and several left turns. I thanked her, turned right, and started out on the correct road — the one in front of the hospital. I took a second right turn and didn't recognize anything. Before long I was hopelessly lost. I prayed for help. The truck driver in front of me seemed to know where he was going so I followed him. He never knew God used him to guide me.

Unfortunately, this isn't an isolated incident. By the time my husband came along, I knew I had a problem. Fortunately, he has a compass embedded in his brain. Though my lack of direction makes no sense to him, he patiently explains over and over about the sun rising in the east and setting in the west…and stuff that's supposed to help me figure it out.

Poor man. He fights a losing battle.

Vacations are particularly challenging. He gives me maps to unfamiliar locations and I usually successfully maneuver us around new cities. When I tell him to turn right and the correct address is on the left, he flips the map over for me. I take it with as much grace as possible. Sometimes I just want to be the one who's right.

The summer my daughter turned seven, we traveled to Williamsburg, Virginia. The section around Colonial Williamsburg is not large so I offered to direct us there without his help. Using the map, I guided him to a parking lot that wasn't where I thought it would be. But it worked; we were within walking distance of the historic attraction.

We left the lot with me holding the trusty map. I expected to see old town stores with wagons nearby. Instead the homes looked modern with cars parked in driveways.

My husband suggested that we stroll to the left.

"I'm the one with map." I shook it for emphasis. "I'll get us there. You don't know where you're going."

I continued to search the area to the right for a side street noted on the map.

My daughter held my hand and skipped along at my side. "Mommy, look. It's one of those old-fashioned ladies." A woman dressed in colonial clothing crossed in front of us. "She probably works at one of the old shops."

"I'll bet you're right. Thanks, honey." I smiled at my daughter. "Excuse me." The stranger glanced up. "Can you direct us to Colonial Williamsburg?"

She blinked and then pointed to the left. My gaze followed her pointing finger to a side street where the old town rose in plain view.

My mouth dropped open. "The map is wrong. How does anyone find this place?"

My husband rubbed his chin. "Is it possible you misread it?"

The suggestion didn't please me, but my track record isn't the best.

He took the map. Starting with the parking lot, he explained where I'd gone wrong.

Maps help folks like me, but they don't trump a keen sense of direction.

~ Sandra Merville Hart

57
White House Calling

"White House calling." The words still ring in my ears and give cause to an irresistible urge to laugh out loud. I had just accepted a marketing position at a world famous Arabian horse ranch; a dream job for a grownup whose worn pages of the book, *Black Beauty*, still took priority on a bookshelf.

My new boss became well known, not only because of the fine quality of horses he bred, but the fact that he rubbed elbows with many political figures and movie stars.

On my first day as a new employee, I was cautioned by his secretary, "Mr. C's private line is always answered by me…and only me. However, none of the phones in the office should ever ring more than two times before they're answered. Mr. C is very strict about this."

I nodded in agreement before I swiveled the desk chair back toward my computer. On beautiful cream-colored linen paper I began to type out the stack of pedigrees I had been given.

Ring. Ring. Ring.

I looked over my shoulder and noticed Mr. C's secretary was not at her desk. The private line had already rung three times. I knew Mr. C. was in his office and I remembered the strict rule about the telephones.

I almost broke a toe as I ran toward the secretary's desk to answer the phone just before the next ring finished.

"Mr. C's office. May I help you?" My breath came in spurts from my exertion.

"White House calling."

I couldn't believe my ears. What kind of a prank call was that? I hesitated only briefly before I said, "Yeah right, and I am Elizabeth Taylor!" I felt a bubble of giggles creep into my throat before I placed the receiver into its cradle. I turned to go back to my desk when I sensed Mr. C's secretary behind me.

"Was that Mr. C's private line ringing?" Her eyebrows came to a peak and she tilted her head sideways.

The giggle that had bubbled up earlier came pouring out of my mouth. "Yes, yes, but you will never believe the prank caller. She said, "White House calling. It only took me a minute before I said, 'Yeah right, and I'm Elizabeth Taylor.'"

The secretary threw her hand up to her forehead. Her face literally blanched white in front of me. She appeared like she might faint.

"That *was* the White House." She immediately sat at her desk and began to dial a number on the phone.

No one had bothered to tell me that my boss was a close personal friend of Ronald Reagan.

My knees wobbled on my way back to my desk. Would they fire me? I felt sick to my stomach. I pulled my chair out and just as the back of my knees hit the seat, I heard Mr. C's voice from his office.

"Yes, yes, she is new. Just hired her yesterday. Poor thing, she must be mortified." Laughter. More laughter.

I folded my arms on the top of my desk and buried my head deeply into them. I wanted to smack my forehead into the hard laminated wood. Mr. C came out of his office a few minutes later. He passed by my desk on his way out the front door to check on one of the foals in a paddock.

"Elizabeth," he said, tapping his fingers on the edge of my desk. "I'll be back in a few minutes. Please don't take any of my calls." He winked at me and stifled a laugh.

After the snickering died down in the office and I recovered from feeling like a complete fool, I vowed to never pick up the private line again…ever.

- Alice Klies

≈ 58 ≈
The Weight of Foolishness

The prodigal son "came to himself" when he started craving pig slop. The prophet Jonah "awakened" as he spat seaweed out of his mouth while entangled in the intestines of a fish. My *what-am-I-doing-here* moment happened in the office of an elementary school, surrounded by alarm bells, copy machines and a multi-line phone system.

It began as a typical day in the school office — phones rang, children arrived late with myriad excuses, and notes going home needed to be written and proofed. Copies had to be made and delivered to each teacher's box. Bus schedules needed to be revised and updated. Medicine was administered to several children and the first-aid cabinet was raided a couple times in the wake of skinned knees.

Then it got busy.

Several school staff were talking on their two-way radios when a piercing noise ripped through the building. I was so busy that morning, I had forgotten about the coming fire drill. I stood motionless in the middle of the office as organized chaos swirled around me.

Lines of children walked past the office window as their teachers worked to keep order. Multiple phone lines continued to light up, the callers clueless to the scheduled drill. In my hands, I carried several files that needed to be returned to storage and documents that had to be copied.

At least a half-dozen tasks needed my immediate attention, but for a few seconds, I couldn't move. *What am I doing here? What is a creative introvert doing in all of this noise?*

I had taken the part-time position a few months prior, with the goal of taking the pressure off what I knew God wanted me to do: write for his glory. In my distorted thinking, if I could earn a few dollars in another job — *any* job — then in theory I could relax and mosey through pretending to be a writer. I could turn out something now and then just to satisfy my creative compulsions and fend off the questions of others.

In fact, I had run from God's call on my life for years. Oh, I had dabbled in putting words on paper, writing an occasional drama script, or poem. But I had lost the joy and passion of being who my Lord designed me to be.

What did it look like to be out of God's will?

Tears. Anxiousness. An unsettled spirit. Excuses. Fear.

Running from God's design left me exhausted and miserable. Each morning, I woke, reached beside the bed, and pulled on the weight of "something's not right." Then I proceeded to wear it while taking on jobs and activities where I thought I could "do some good."

In *My Utmost for His Highest*, Oswald Chambers warns against this very thing:

> Practical work may be a competitor against abandonment to God, because practical work is based on this argument — Remember how useful you are here, or — Think how much value you would be in that particular type of work. That attitude does not put Jesus Christ as the Guide as to where we should go, but our judgment as to where we are of most use.

I may have been doing some good, but I wasn't fulfilling my intended role in God's Kingdom work. I had shut myself off from everything that brought me joy in serving, and that was writing, dreaming, and creating. Instead of finding my strength and peace in Christ and his plans, I succumbed to fear and spent years living a paralyzed life.

It was time to stop running.

That night, this broken woman sobbed until there were no tears left. My husband pulled me close and whispered, "Are you ready to do what God planned for you?"

There was risk involved and I was afraid. But at that moment, it seemed more reckless to keep running than to step out in faith and trust in my Lord's purposes. I was tired of being the foolish servant, squandering my talent. I wanted my Master to be proud of me and rejoice in my obedience.

It was time for me to come home to the heart of God.

In faith, I stepped away from a position that God had designed for someone else. In faith, I placed my hand in his, eager to begin this new journey of living my calling.

Recently I read a rare journal entry from my time of running. I had penned it with the unsteady script of sadness. I'd written, "There is most likely an incredible amount of joy on the other side of this fear."

Yes! Praise God, yes.

- Leigh Ann Thomas

I was ready for an appointment and wanted to look my best. I decided to check the mirror for the last time before leaving. Yes, the eyes were lined smoothly, the black mascara lushly lengthened my lashes as promised on the tube, eyebrows dusted with black powder, cheeks revealed a healthy rose tone, the brushed-on foundation looked smooth and natural, the lips alluring with a glow to compliment any smile. Ah, yes! But…maybe I should apply just a tad more above my lips to better conceal those little grooves that appear over time. Therefore, I picked up the brush, tapped it into the makeup, gently moving it from one side to the other of my upper lip…which left a perfect line of nicely trimmed black mustache.

- Yvonne

59
Focus Lost and Found

I stood at the counter, sponge in hand, cleaning up the dinner mess. I caught myself sighing again. A busy schedule left me with an empty energy tank. I grumbled, "This stove has seen better days. What a chore to clean."

A snippet of a Bible verse came to mind. I recalled the first part well enough: Don't be weary in doing good, for we will...if we don't quit. We will what? I tried to think of the missing words. "Find rest"? That didn't sound right. "Find hope"? Nope. Maybe it said, "gain strength." Sure, that's what I needed — strength to keep going. "Be rewarded?" I liked the sound of that. I'd look it up later.

By the time I finished cleaning the kitchen, the verse was forgotten. I remembered the next morning and hunted in my concordance under "weary." Shocked, I read Galatians 6:9: Let us not become weary in doing good, for at the proper time we will reap a harvest if we do not give up. Reap a harvest?

That sounded like weary work right there. I hoped the verse promised strength, rest, or reward. Ouch. How out of touch I felt. I wanted my way, not God's. Not to mention my injured pride — all that scripture memorization for naught. Hiding God's word in my heart isn't much use if I can't find it.

Was my eye so fixed on the prize of heaven that I'd become shortsighted or lazy about the duties in the here and now? Or maybe I've conformed to a culture that says, "You deserve a break today." In our busyness, losing focus comes easily.

Realizing we're off track can be embarrassing, but it's the first step to getting back on. It took a weak moment to remind me there's kingdom work to be done, not just rest and rewards.

A closer look at Galatians chapter 6 gives a glimpse of God's generosity. He says if we press on in doing good, we'll be rewarded with fruit. If we sow to please the Spirit, we'll reap a bountiful harvest. The gain isn't based on working harder or being super talented. Just. Don't. Give. Up.

Not that God disallows down time. He knows our needs and promises to restore our souls (Psalm 23:2–3). Tiredness, a full calendar, or discouragement causes us to lose focus or, worse yet, to quit. That's just what our enemy delights in. So run to the Lord. He says that those who are weary find rest (Matthew 11:28). When we're yoked to Jesus, doing good is less a burden and more a privilege.

Was it an epic fail to momentarily overlook God's big picture or forget a Bible verse? Maybe not.

Yet how quickly His word sets us straight when we let it. As we have the chance, let's keep doing good. The harvest reaped will bring glory to God, and He assures us that one day we'll get a nice, long rest.

~ Lynn Lilja

♦ 60 ♦
Me? Have a Stupid Moment?

When the idea of an anthology of stupid moments was discussed in our writing group, my memory politely stood and left the room. I watched it detach from my body much like an apparition and float away. As it exited the building carrying with it the recollection of less than savory moments in my past, I wondered why everyone else in the room had a story to tell and I had nothing. What had my memory taken away when it escaped?

Months later I was standing in my kitchen in the middle of a phone conversation with a friend, talking about various people we knew, when I felt a cold shudder as if someone had walked into the room and left the door open to the frigid air outside. Glancing toward the door I saw my memory had returned and was poking its head tentatively through the kitchen door as a long forgotten thought scampered across the room and through my mind knocking the breath from me.

A long time ago in a town not so far away I was having lunch with a friend at a quite popular local restaurant, the kind where the thick wooden backs of the booths were too tall to see over the top. We were having a spirited conversation about people we knew as we laughed and gossiped and felt secure that what we shared was just between the two of us.

The food was good, the atmosphere festive, and the gossip therapy refreshing. It was good to let all those secrets out. Near the end of our meal, the patrons behind us slid from their booth and stood to leave. As I glanced toward them red heat radiated up my neck and across my face as I recognized a woman as one of the people about whom my friend and I had said some unflattering things.

The woman smiled at me, nodded a greeting, and asked how I was doing. My fork slipped from my fingers and clanged against the tabletop as I mumbled a greeting and forced a smile. Though she smiled I could see that she had overheard. How stupid I was to think my negative words about another were safe and could cause no harm. What an embarrassing way to learn a hard lesson. I desperately wanted to disappear into the restaurant wall. In my kitchen the evening the long ago memory found its way back to me, I realized I had blocked the incident from my mind all those years, and I had gridlocked the lesson it meant to teach me. I ended the current conversation abruptly feeling ashamed as I thought about some harsh verses in the book of Matthew.

How could evil men like you speak what is good and right? For a man's heart determines his speech. A good man's speech reveals the rich treasures within him. An evil-hearted man is filled with venom, and his speech reveals it. (Matthew 12:34–35 TLB)

My heart filled with venom? Unfathomable. Those words were not how I would describe myself and yet, the truth had revealed who I really was. I didn't want to face it then, but because of the task the authors had been given for this project, my brain — working behind the scenes — unleashed that moment of sheer absurdity and embarrassment.

With that in mind as I stood in my kitchen that evening still doing the same thing I had for years, I finally realized I was not who I said I was and I needed to make a change. From that day forward I made a decision to have compassion for people rather than to allow venom into my heart and subsequently my words. As Christians we are called to be encouragers and our words a healing balm, not a sword to inflict more pain.

It's a process, and daily I am becoming more aware of the words I share. Today my mantra is to spread words that entertain, encourage and inspire. And I hope to use what I've learned to motivate others to do the same.

~ Fran Lee Strickland

༻ 61 ༺
The Closet Prayer

Several years ago, someone in the household was watching a television program about surprise reunions, such as adopted persons finding biological parents, friends or relatives reunited following long absences, etc. That particular day, I'd stood for a moment watching a segment of the show about reuniting sisters who had been adopted and hadn't seen each other since they were toddlers.

After three young women were introduced, the host said, "When we return, we will find out which one is the real sister."

I didn't really care, so I returned to my office-bedroom where I had been preparing the Sunday school lesson I was to teach. I took a look, and felt it was ready. Prayer time came next.

During that time, we had a family situation that was a closet kind of prayer. In a corner of the bedroom, converted into my office, was a small closet space, the size of its door, where one could stand. To the right was the wall. In front, upon walking in, were shelves. The left was slanted space over the stairs, beyond and down from my office.

The closet had no light and was a perfect place for those prayers I considered to be more dire, and thus, required more than just closing my eyes. I walked into the closet, closed the door, stood in the dark (although I'm scared of spiders and knew they must be in there!) and began my heart-wrenching prayer.

While in the middle of a sentence to the One who could perform miracles, or at least give peace of mind or take away the burden, I heard, "Now we will find out who is the real sister."

With a quick turn, I grasped that doorknob, slung open the door, and ran into the living room to find out who was the real sister.

I stood there, watched the sisters embrace. It wasn't even about whether or not they would be reunited. Only a matter of which one. "Which one" really didn't matter to me.

Then mortification set in.

My eyes slowly turned toward the doorway. I turned and slunk down that hall, reluctantly entered the office and willed myself into the closet. I couldn't even remember what the first part of my sentence to God had been.

But I knew what my prayer had to be! So I shut myself up into that dark space and stood and with all sincerity, prayed, "Lord, bring on the spiders. Let them have at me."

At least, that cured me of being afraid the spiders might attack me. I deserved every eight-eyed stare, every crawly leg and every bite I might get.

~ Yvonne Lehman

❧ 62 ❧
A Place of Trust

Throughout the devotional, *Magnificent Prayer*, one of the names you see frequently is that of Oswald Chambers. Of all the prominent Christians I've read about, Chambers alone has the unique situation of being used by God far more after his death than when he was alive.

He died suddenly at age 43 in Egypt where he was ministering to British troops. Later, his best writings were edited into books, the most notable of which has been the classic daily devotional, *My Utmost for His Highest*. The following entries from Chambers' journal give us a peek at the man who would die before he saw what God would do with him.

> *Portrush, Dec. 5, 1908.* The great power and groan of the mighty sea seems to awaken that longing loneliness of the prophet about me for God. I am hungry with a vast desire for Him. As I go about for Him other lives seem to me to get clearer and clearer, but I find I dare not look to anyone to understand mine.
>
> This is not pride, but the call is on me, intolerably strong at times. I am full of joy always, but a tremendous sorrow seems to be interwoven with it all. I seem to hear Him, but still I am sense and ark to His meaning. I wish He would take me into His counsel or let me live on the lower level. I am just sensitive enough to His Spirit to know that we are on the eve of new things, not the revival that every one seems to be talking about, that does not appeal to me. Nor is it the Second Coming. I know He is coming again and coming again soon. But there is something He wants me to see and know, and I seem stupid. I can feel intuitively the Spirit of God striving with me.
>
> *Jan. 8, 1909.* It came so clearly to me that in all ventures for God I had to go in faith, and now I do the same. It will be a great and joyful thing to see how God will open up the way. I never see my way. I know God Who guides so I fear nothing. I have never far-seeing plans, only confident trust.

There is much to be said for planning ahead under God's direction. But sometimes God directs otherwise. A young Oswald Chambers had a call on his life. Yet it was an indistinct call that drove him to repeatedly ask God to let him know what that call was to mean.

And then in the January entry in his journal, Oswald says that in all ventures for God, he had to go in faith. He anticipated only that God would open up a way in response to his prayers.

Perhaps the reason that God didn't share His plan with Oswald or give him far-seeing plans was that Oswald would die soon. And yet, incredibly, God's plan for the young missionary was *extremely* far-reaching. More than a century later, Christians around the world are daily reading the best-selling devotional book of all time, compiled after his death by his wife, Biddy. That book is *My Utmost for His Highest* and it was the posthumous answer to Oswald's prayer. God has used Oswald Chambers far, far more after his death in ways he could never have imagined.

It was good that Oswald Chambers came to a place of trust that God would answer his prayers and use him. It is good when we do the same.

~ *Nick Harrison*

֍

Whether we, as Oswald Chambers, "seem stupid" or are stupid,
act stupid in silly or serious ways,
the most stupid thing we can do is ignore and reject
our Lord and Savior, Jesus Christ.
There is nothing more intelligent than coming to Jesus like a trusting child
to give our hearts and lives to him,
for that has earthly and eternal significance.

God so loved the world
that he gave his only Son,
so that everyone who believes in him
will not perish
but have eternal life.

John 3:16 NLT

About the Authors

Gloria Anderson is a wife, mother and grandmother. She is the author of *Beauty from My Ashes*. She was born and continues to live in the beautiful mountains of western North Carolina. She serves Christ as a women's Bible study teacher in her church and leading in worship through singing with her choir. Her passion is helping women, especially hurting women, find the forgiveness, hope, healing, peace and growth that she found through a personal relationship with Jesus Christ. She loves to write, teach and speak to ladies.

Joye Atkinson was born in South Carolina and has written poetry for 30 years. She writes from personal experiences and it is her prayer that the words God gives her will be a blessing to many. Her first book of poetry, *From the Heart*, is a recent publication. She is working on her second book. She declares, "To God be the glory for all he has done!"

Karen Nolan Bell started writing in her front porch swing, surrounded by the coal-filled mountains of Kentucky. Karen's education includes an area in fine arts, acting, creative writing, and art. Her writing credits include stories in the anthology *Relief Notes*, newspaper articles, literary journals, newsletters, blogs, promotional materials for non-profits, dramas for churches and schools, and commercials/public service announcements for Christian radio. Her first novel, set in Appalachia and with a touch of mystery, has yet to be published. Karen currently resides in Georgia and has one awesome adult son. You can contact her on Facebook.

Mason K. Brown's many writings have been published in six volumes of *Chicken Soup for the Sou; Guideposts; When God Makes Lemonade; RAIN Magazine 2013, 2014, 2015, and 2016; Vista; The Secret Place; The Mother's Heart* magazine; *Help! I'm A Parent; God Makes Lemonade; CAP Connection; Apple Hill Cider Press; Seeds of…A Collection of Writings by Pacific Northwest Authors,* and others. Her latest work is included in *Jesus Encounters.* Until 2016, Mason K. Brown previously wrote under the name of Karen R. Hessen. Visit her website: Karenrhesssen.com.

Roger E. Bruner worked as a teacher, job counselor, and programmer analyst before retiring to pursue his dream of writing Christian fiction full time. A guitarist and songwriter, he is active in his church choir, plays bass on the praise team, and plays guitar at the weekly nursing home ministry. Roger also enjoys reading, web design, mission trips, photography, and spending time with his wonderful wife, Kathleen. Roger has two young adult novels, *Found in Translation* and *Lost in Dreams*, and a speculative satire, *The Devil and Pastor Gus*. He also has nine unpublished novels. He published two small books of shorter writings, *Yesterday's Blossoms* and *More of Yesterday's Blossoms.* Learn more about Roger and his writings at togerbruner.com

Elsie H. Brunk and her husband of 57 years have four children, 12 grandchildren and four great-grandchildren. Her devotions and articles have been published in

Christian Parenting Today, Live, The Family Digest, Standard, The Secret Place and other periodicals. Her book, *Streams of Living Water for a Thirsty Soul* is available as an e-book. Elise's stories, "Grandchild Journal — Legacy of Love," and "The Roses" are included in *Precious, Precocious Moments*. "A Fresh New Christmas" is in *More Christmas Moments*. Visit Elsie on her website: elsiebrunk.com.

Janet Bryant Campbell is a freelance writer and playwright. Her favorite plays are those co-written with her son, Nathan Campbell. They include *Locked Away, All That Glitters*, the outdoor drama *Martyrs and Mayhem*, and a dinner theater production, *Mystery at the Manger*. Janet, a dog lover, is owned by a six-pound Pomeranian. After her Pomeranian was diagnosed with the autoimmune disease, Immune Mediated Hemolytic Anemia, or IMHA, in 2013, Janet has focused on writing articles that help other pet owners deal with this disease and to raise awareness among pet owners. Janet is currently working on turning stories she wrote for her son as a child into a series of children's picture books. She is also diving into her favorite genre, and has started work on a mystery novel.

Rebecca Carpenter writes at her lake retreat in Florida. After retiring from teaching elementary school, she and her husband traveled the world for missions and pleasure. Experiences with her granddaughters, traveling, and nature inspire her writings. Her articles have appeared in *Clubhouse* magazine, *Posh Parenting, Christmas Moments, Celebrating Christmas with…Memories, Poetry, and Good Food*, and several local publications. After losing her husband and both parents within months, she wrote page after page of her grief journey. Forty of those devotionals are available in her book *Ambushed by Glory*. Visit her blog, *Inspirations from Life*, at rebeccacarpenter.blogspot.com.

Joann M. Claypoole is the author of *DoveStories*, a children's chapter book series for ages 6–8, and *The Gardener's Helpers*. She has written a children's devotional book, *Coo Says You Are Loved* (ages 2–5). Her story, "A Picture in the Sky," is included in *Divine Moments*. Joann co-wrote the television documentary script for *My Last Hope*, hosted by Candace Cameron-Bure, for National House of Hope. Her inspirational prayers were featured on Clickandpray.com and have been compiled into two books, *All I Am* and *Everything to Me*. She also writes songs, voiceovers, plays, articles, and blogs. Joann is a member of the Christian Writers Guild, Word Weavers International, Society of Children's Book Writers an Illustrators (SCBWI), Mt. Dora SCBWI Critique group, and Amhurst Writers and Critique Group. She is a wife, mother of four sons, Numi to three grandbabies, doggie-mom of two, and salon/spa owner in sunny Florida. Joann serves local and international missions and loves to sing on the praise and worship leading team at her local church.

Sharon Blackstock Dobbs has been sharing her poetry and prose with family and friends for five decades. Sharon downsized her home but not her life. She wants to share her poetry and prose with a larger following. Sending her words into the world just as she has her two sons, she prays that they will be an encouragement to others.

Susan Dollyhigh is a freelance writer and speaker. She is a contributing author in *Spirit and Heart: A Devotional Journey; Faith and Finances: In God We Trust; The Ultimate Christian Living; God Still Meets Needs,* and *I Believe in Heaven.* Susan's articles have appeared in *Connection Magazine, Exemplify Magazine, Mustard Seed Ministry, P31 Woman, The Upper Room* and *The Secret Place.*

Dorothy Floyd has made her home in, Georgia for over 20 years. She finds life as a single mom and a special education teacher both challenging and rewarding. In the next few years, Dorothy plans to retire from teaching and publish her collection of devotional stories taken from life experiences.

Theresa Jenner Garrido was born in the beautiful Pacific Northwest and spent the first nine years of her life on an island in Puget Sound. With no neighborhood children nearby, she depended on imaginary people to keep her company until the much anticipated summer months when her best friend and cousin came to visit. Theresa attended the University of Washington, received a B.A. in English, and spent the next 20+ years teaching middle school language arts, drama, and social studies before retiring "early." Now she's happy to indulge her wild imagination and passionate love of history and share these foibles with others, including her husband, Jerry, her extended family, and a rescue pup and stray black cat. Theresa has made her home in Missouri, Georgia, and North Carolina but currently resides in South Carolina. When not at the computer or in the laundry room, she enjoys traveling and poking her nose into strange and mysterious places.

Tommy Scott Gilmore, III, a gifted speaker and motivational leader, is Executive Director of Changing Lives Ministry in Asheville, North Carolina. His life has not been boring. To experience poverty, he spent a winter's month in Boston's ghetto with only 50¢ in his pocket. He rode a bicycle over 20,000 miles through 20 states and 12 countries, climbed St. Goddard Pass in the Swiss Alps and cheated death on several occasions by surviving quicksand, numerous auto accidents and threats on his life from his preaching. He is happily married to Sandra Gault Gilmore formerly of South Carolina. They have three grown daughters, Lindsey, Brittany and Meghan, and two grandchildren, Sarah Grace and Victoria. You can find his life-changing testimony on his website: changinglivesministry.info.

Dianna Beamis Good is a retired English teacher of 25 years. She has been journaling and writing for years mostly for her own enjoyment of reliving and discovering life. She was encouraged to join Northern Arizona's Word Weavers and has appreciated the talent of those around her. Dianna has been blessed with her husband and best friend of 36 years, two grown children, and four beautiful grandchildren.

Nick Harrison is an author and editor from Oregon. He has written 10 books, including *Magnificent Prayer, His Victorious Indwelling,* and *Power in the Promises.* Visit his website: nickharrisonnooks.com.

Sandra Merville Hart's Civil War romance, *A Stranger On My Land,* is a 2015 International Reader's Choice Award Finalist and 2016 Christian Small Publisher

Book of the Year Finalist. She serves as Assistant Editor for *DevoKids* and publishes history-related articles on the site. She is the column writer for "History in the Making" at *AlmostanAuthor*. She contributed to several books including *Jesus Encounters* and *Spoken Moments*. She has written for several publications and blogs including *The Secret Place*, *Harpstring*, *Splickety Magazine*, *Pockets*, and *Christian Devotions*. Whenever possible, she and her husband travel to the locations in her books to discover lesser-known facts. She loves to research American history and incorporate what she learns into her stories.

Helen L. Hoover enjoys sewing, reading, knitting, and traveling. She and her husband are retired, live in Northwest Arkansas and volunteer at a Christian college. They are blessed with two grown children, four grandchildren and four great-grandchildren. Helen's devotions and personal stories are published in books and Christian handout papers.

Lillian Humphries has been the publisher for her church's Christian ladies newsletter for two years. She speaks to Christian ladies groups, has been a ladies Bible class teacher, and teaches teen girls. You can follow Lillian at her blog, connectedchristianwomen.blogspot.com, Twitter, and Facebook. She has three books "under construction" as she works on articles for magazines. She has written a children's book for her grandchildren, *Meme's got the Buttons*. Lillian is a member of American Christian Fiction Writers and ACFW-SC the South Carolina Chapter. She has contributed her stories to *Divine Moments* and *Christmas Moments*. A transplant from Florida, she moved to South Carolina in 2001. She is married to Doug Humphries, whom she met online. They recently celebrated their ninth wedding anniversary. Together they have two daughters and two sons, and 10 grandchildren who are the loves of their lives.

Terri Kelly is the author of *Mary Slessor: Missionary Mother*. As a writer she has contributed to several books, including *Divine Moments*, *Faith and Family*, and *Spirit and Heart*. Terri has published articles in *The Kids' Ark* magazine, *Clubhouse*, *WHOA Magazine*, and numerous online publications. Her blog, terribkelly.com, addresses issues teachers deal with on a daily basis. She teaches at writing conferences and assists with the Asheville Christian Writers Conference in North Carolina.

Alice Klies is a freelance writer and member of Northern Arizona's Word Weavers International. She has been published in *WordSmith Journal*. Her stories, "Just Us Girls" and "The Dog Did What?" are published in *Chicken Soup for the Soul*. Other stories appearing in anthologies include "Grandfather, Father and Me," "Grandmother, Mother and Me," "God Still Meets Needs," and "Friends of Faith." Still another, "Angels on Earth" is published in *Guideposts*. Alice is currently writing a memoir.

Barbara Latta is a freelance writer whose passion is to share how the grace of God can free us from the rules of religious tradition. Her articles, devotions, and poems have been published in several newspapers, magazines, and websites. She writes a monthly column for the *Pike Journal-Reporter*. She is a board member of East Metro

Atlanta Christian Writers. She enjoys riding motorcycles with her Harley husband, and their biker travels are the inspiration for her blog: barbaralatta.blogspot.com.

David A. Lehman's poem "Today It Rained Gorillas," written when he was seven years old, and his short story, "The Accident," written when he was nine years old, are published in *Precious, Precocious Moments*. He is author of technical writing. He is a pastor and educator, has three children, and lives in North Carolina.

Yvonne Lehman is author of 57 novels. She founded, and directed for 25 years, the Blue Ridge Mountains Christian Writers Conference. She now directs the Blue Ridge Novelist Retreat held annually in October at Ridgecrest Conference Center in North Carolina. She lives in North Carolina with her beautiful furry blond and white Pomeranian, Rigel, named after a Titanic survivor. In addition to the *Moments* series, her latest books include a novella, *Have Dress Will Marry*, in the *Heart of a Cowboy* collection, and a compilation, *Writing Right to Success*, by 25 authors about their journey to success and craft articles for writers. Her popular, 50th book is *Hearts that Survive — A Novel of the Titanic*, which she signs periodically at the Titanic Museum in Pigeon Forge, Tennessee.

Lynn Lilja's book, *Get Cooking*, sells great at her speaking engagements. She's been published in *Christian Devotions* and on Awana's blog. As regional speaker trainer for Stonecroft Ministries, she hosts Faith Stories workshops for speakers and edits manuscripts for Stonecroft speakers.

Diana Leagh Matthews is a vocalist, speaker, writer, life coach, and genealogist. She is a Christian Communicators and Christian Devotions Boot Camp graduate. She has been published in several anthologies, including *Spoken Moments* and *More Christmas Moments*. She currently resides in South Carolina. Visit her website, dianaleaghmatthews,com and her blog, *A Look Thru Time*, at alookthrutime.com

Andrea Merrell is Associate Editor for Christian Devotions Ministries and Lighthouse Publishing of the Carolinas. She is also a freelance editor, teaches workshops at writers' conferences, and has been published in numerous anthologies and online venues. Andrea is a graduate of Christian Communicators and a finalist in the 2015 USA Best Book Awards. She is the author of *Murder of a Manuscript* and *Praying for the Prodigal*. Visit her online at andreamerrell.com and thewriteediting.com.

Maggie Micoff is wife of a wonderful man named Dan, mother of four children, eight grandchildren, six great-grandchildren, and pet-parent to six cats and two dogs (Rose and Jack). She is a published poet and article writer, loves crocheting, painting, sewing, decorating, creating unique things, and has her own business making handcrafted jewelry. She lives in a quaint town nestled in the lower thumb area of Michigan that divides Canada from the United States and stretches from Port Huron Michigan to Lake St. Clair. She claims to be a Titaniac (Titanic fanatic) who has a collection mainly of James Cameron Titanic movie memorabilia including Rose's ensembles, steamer truck, heart of the ocean necklaces, butterfly combs and some of the scale models of the bench, Adirondack chair, life boat, etc. She was recently voted a board member on her local Historical Commission, is chairperson of Great Lakes Titanic Society, and is gathering funds for a Michigan Titanic Memorial to be placed in Marine City in memory of the 70 Michigan-bound passengers aboard the *Titanic*. Last but not least, she says, "I love Jesus Christ, my Lord and Savior! Don't leave Earth without Him!"

Marybeth Mitcham holds a B.S. in biology, is completing her M.P.H. in nutrition, and currently works as a community educator. She is a freelance author whose writings have been published in several anthologies, in *Celebrate Life* magazine, in *Thriving Family* magazine, and online. She has been a guest on the *Chris Fabry Live* radio show, discussing her article "*My Magnum Opus.*" Marybeth lives with her family in the Southern Adirondack region of New York, where she can often be found hiking mountains, riding motorcycles, or hovering near the woodstove in her spare time.

Vicki H. Moss is Contributing Editor and past Editor-at-Large for *Southern Writers Magazine*. A columnist for the *American Daily Herald*, she's also a poet, a Precept Ministries Leader, a Christian Communicators graduate, and author of *How to Write for Kids' Magazines* and *Writing with Voice*. She has written for *Hopscotch* and *Boy's Quest* magazines for the last decade in addition to being published in *Christmas Moments, Divine Moments* and *Precious, Precocious Moments,* SouthWest Writer's *SouthWest Sage, Country Woman, In the City, Borderlines,* Scotland's *Thistle Blower*, and *I Believe in Heaven*. She was selected to be a presenter of her fiction and creative nonfiction short stories for three consecutive Southern Women Writers Conferences. Vicki is a speaker and faculty member for writers conferences. She is also a photographer who does book styling to help authors promote novels, poetry, and nonfiction. For more information visit her online at livingwaterfiction.com.

Shelley Pierce is a pastor's wife, mom to four, grandmother and author. Her passion is encouraging folks to remain faithful in all seasons of life. She enjoys serving as Director of Preschool and Children's Ministries at Towering Oaks Baptist Church in Greeneville, Tennessee. Her writing includes numerous children's curriculum with LifeWay Christian Resources and a column titled "Hope Etc." in *Christian Online* magazine. She is published through *The Upper Room* devotional guide, *Power for Living* and in various magazine articles. Shelley strives to look for God's hand in everything she does, choosing to have fun each day because life is too short to focus on the negatives. Connect with her on Facebook, Twitter, and her personal blog, shellleypaperbackwriter.blogspot.com.

Debbie Presnell is a published author, national speaker and workshop presenter, co-founder of Shine! Ministries, and partner with the Polished Conference LLC. She has an online Bible study on Facebook, teaches Bible study in her church, and blogs at *Living Life Together*. Debbie has written *Shine! Radiating the Love of God*, a Bible study designed exclusively for young women ages 13-18. Additionally, she has articles in the *Divine Moments* series and is a monthly contributor to *Refined Magazine*. She would love to speak at your next women's event, teen event, or college where she brings an inspirational message to teachers in training titled "A Christian Perspective for an Inspirational Classroom." Debbie is married and has three adult children. She travels from Asheville, North Carolina. Visit her website: debbiepresnell.com, or visit her page on Facebook: https://www.facebook.com/shineministriesnc.

Colleen L. Reece describes herself as an ordinary person with an extraordinary God. Raised in a home without electricity or running water but filled with love for God and family, Colleen learned to read by kerosene lamplight and dreamed of someday writing a book. God has multiplied her "someday" book into *150 Books You Can Trust*, with six million copies sold.

Toni Armstrong Sample retired from Pennsylvania to South Carolina at the end of a successful career as a Human Resource executive, and owner of a management consulting, training, and development firm. A published author in journals and magazines, in 2014 she celebrated the release of her first three novels of inspiration, intrigue and romance, *The Glass Divider*, *Transparent Web of Dreams*, and *Distortion*. Toni is a Christian retreat leader, conference speaker, Bible study facilitator, and commission artist.

Gloria Spears lives in the Tennessee foothills of the Great Smoky Mountains. Gloria is a freelance writer of self-help articles, poems and devotions. She runs her errands and works with her decorating business during the day and writes in evenings. Gloria has been journaling and writing for enjoyment since her teen years. Her writing is inspirational for those going through difficult times and divorce. Gloria has been the speaker at numerous networking conferences for more than a decade. For several years, she was the editor of a vacation newsletter in their family business.

Cindy Sproles is cofounder of Christian Devotions Ministries. She serves as the Executive Editor of *Christian Devotions* online and is the Devotional Acquisitions Editor for Lighthouse Publishing of the Carolinas. Cindy is a conference teacher, speaker, and mentor. Cindy's devotions are published in Christian newspapers across the eastern seaboard. She's the author of two non-fiction books and *Mercy's Rain*, an Appalachian Novel. Visit her website: cindysproles.om.

Nate Stevens is a "missionary kid" who grew up in a Christian home and church. He has enjoyed a 30-year banking career in a variety of leadership roles. He writes online devotions for Christian Devotions Ministries, devotions for his home church in North Carolina, and articles for several publications. His book, *Matched 4 Marriage – Meant 4 Life,* is available at all major book retailers. His article, "A Shooting Star When You Need One" is an excerpt from his next book, *Deck Time in the Storm,* which is currently in production. He speaks at conferences, seminars and Bible study groups for singles, young adults, young marrieds, and youth. He lives in North Carolina and is an active dad with his two awesome kids, Melissa and Mitchell. Contact and book information may be found online at: natestevens.net.

Fran Lee Strickland serves as treasurer of the American Christian Fiction Writers chapter of South Carolina, is a member of Blue Ridge Writers group, and is working on her first suspense novel, *Roots That Run Deep*. She is a contributor to three nonfiction anthologies: *Divine Moments*, *Christmas Moments* and *Spoken Moments*. She is mother of Jake. Loves intrigue, chocolate, and coffee! She blogs about faith and writing at scatteringwordsandsowingseeds.blogspot.com.

Barb Suiter loves words and enjoys putting them together to make sense out of a crazy world. Her blog, *ajourneytonow.me* includes spiritual truths learned from the birds at the window, weeds, marriage, or any one of a multitude of passions. She has written devotionals for *Christian Devotions*. After living and serving in missions in Western Europe for 10 years she and her husband of 52 years now live in middle Tennessee. They are blessed with 13 grandchildren.

Ann Tatlock is a novelist and children's book author. She also serves as managing editor of Heritage Beacon, the historical fiction imprint of Lighthouse Publishing of the Carolinas. A three-time Christy Award winner, she enjoys helping aspiring writers hone their craft by teaching and mentoring at various writers' conferences. Ann lives with her husband in North Carolina. Their daughter is a student at North Carolina State.

Leigh Ann Thomas is a Jesus follower, wife, mom, Grammy, and Peanut M&M aficionado. She loves to motivate others to reach higher and to seek God's best. Since taking a sword to her writing fears, she has signed a contract to publish an inspirational book for mothers of the bride, become a columnist ay almostanauthor.com, contributed to several devotional collections, and was a finalist in the *Southern Writers Magazine* 2015 Short Story contest. Leigh Ann's blog, *Heart Undivided*, encourages others to live full lives in Christ. Connect with her on Facebook, Twitter, or her blog, leighathomas.com.

Donna Collins Tinsley is a sister among you who wants to bring a word of comfort and hope to your day. She gives praise to the Lord Jesus Christ for His healing power and breaking the chains that once held her. She is a sometimes hormonally challenged wife, mother and grandmother, lives in Florida, and has been included in several magazines and many book compilations. Her devotions have featured on CBN.com. She is a contributor to Christian Devotions Ministries, and has written blurbs for *Thriving Family* and *Publishing Syndicate Newsletter*. She is a lover of the Lord Jesus Christ. Find her on Facebook, or at *A Sister Among You*, thornrose7.blogspot.com.

Audrey Tyler grew up in a Christian home and church. She is a contributing writer for her church newsletter. Audrey received her Bachelor of Arts degree from the University of South Carolina Upstate, and a Master of Science degree from Southern Wesleyan University. Audrey lives in South Carolina with her husband.

Jan Westmark is the editor of *Sideline Magazine*, an equestrian magazine sold in Barnes and Noble and available athorse shows throughout the country. Jan teaches a women's Sunday school class at Biltmore Baptist Church in Asheville, North Carolina and is a ministry partner in Shine! Ministries. Having lived most of her life in Florida, Jan is thrilled to have escaped the heat and to be living in the mountains — a little closer to Heaven!

Kathy Whirity is a syndicated newspaper columnist who shares her sentimental musings on family life. She is the author of *Life Is a Kaleidoscope*, a compilation of her most popular columns. Visit her website kathywhirity.com.

Dr. Rhett H. Wilson, Sr. pastors the Spring Church in Laurens, South Carolina. He enjoys life with his wife, Tracey, and their three children, Hendrix, Anna-Frances, and Dawson. The Wilsons explore waterfalls in the Carolinas, tube down mountain streams, and look forward to March Madness basketball each year. Rhett likes reading legal thrillers and Southern fiction, writing, and listening to country, classical, and Broadway music. Rhett and Tracey have released two CDs, *Lead Me On* and *Offered Praises*. He is writing a book titled *Seven Words to Pray for My Family*. Rhett is available to speak or sing at your church. Visit his blog, *Faith, Family, and Freedom*, at rhettwilson.blogspot.com.

Debra DuPree Williams is a classically trained lyric-coloratura soprano, but her first love is southern Gospel. She began writing when she was a young girl and finished her first novel when she was in the seventh grade. Her essay, *A Tribute to Shan Palmer*, appeared in the online magazine *Dead Mule School of Southern Literature*. She is a member of SCBWI and ACFW. At the 2015 Autumn in the Mountains Novel Retreat, her unpublished cozy mystery, *Grave Consequences*, won second place for best book proposal. When she isn't busy writing, she can be found chasing an elusive ancestor, either through online sources or in country graveyards. She enjoys painting, quilting, or cooking up something totally southern. She has been married to Jim for 43 years. They are the proud parents of four sons, Ken, Christopher, Adam, and Daniel, one amazing daughter-in-law, Cecili, and two beautiful granddaughters, Piper and Emerson. She and Jim live in North Carolina.

Jean Wilund is a Bible teacher and award-winning writer, passionate about coffee and comedy, but mostly about leading others to discover the life-changing truths in God's Word. Her articles have been published in *Clubhouse* and *Clubhouse Jr.*, in several other magazines, and on various websites, including *Guideposts*. She is president of the Lexington, South Carolina Chapter of Word Weavers International, Inc., and a member of Toastmasters, SCBWI, and Palmetto Christian Writers Network. She enjoys connecting with readers on her award-winning blog, *Join the Journey* (jeanwilund.com), as well as on other social media. She lives in South Carolina with her husband Larry. Their three grown children live scattered around the country.

www.ingramcontent.com/pod-product-compliance
Lightning Source LLC
Chambersburg PA
CBHW060534100426
42743CB00009B/1529